Believing God for Work
Strategies and Scriptures
for Job Seekers

by LeDene Lewis

Includes

Ten Commandments
for a Successful Job Search

IMAGES

Chicago, Illinois

First Edition, First Printing

Front cover illustration by Harold Carr

Copyright © 2007 by LeDene Lewis

Printed in the United States of America

10-Digit ISBN #: 1-934155-05-5
13-Digit ISBN #: 9 781934 155059

TABLE OF CONTENTS

Section I: In the Beginning

Section 2: Powering Up for Work

Section 3: Success Strategies/Corresponding Power Scriptures

iv

Believing God for Work
is dedicated…

To my mother, Florence, for modeling a strong work ethic for her children long before we discovered the biblical principles;

To my daughters, Jessica and Walonda, for their laughter; belief in my ability to succeed; helping to keep me to the task of writing—each in her own way—and for their constant support and love and bringing out the best in me;

To my brother, James, a born survivor and Christian warrior who always provides encouraging support;

To Jesse Harrington, Jr., for his consistent willingness to lend a helping hand regardless of the need or personal cost to himself —a true champion of Christ;

To Sandy, Marta and Gerald Scruggs, for having faith in me and this project when it was yet without form;

To my readers —may you find encouragement and empowerment in the biblical principles and scriptures within these pages to find jobs.

May Matthew 22:29 never be said
of Christian or other faith-seeking job seekers:

*Jesus answered and said unto them,
"Ye do err not knowing the scriptures,
nor the power of God."*

Section 1:
In The Beginning

Part 1

Who Should Read This Book and Why

WHO: *Believing God for Work* was written for you, dear reader, to provide biblically sound encouragement to help empower those of you who:

1. Wonder if you can expect godly prayers for new jobs to be answered
2. Have lost your jobs through your own fault or through the fault of another
3. Feel too young or too old to attract employers
4. Want to work in order to free yourselves from a welfare/public assistance system
5. Are afraid of the interviewing process
6. Have a variety of fears about the job search process in general
7. Need encouragement to continue to job search after a string of rejections
8. Have a criminal past and feel no one will want to hire you
9. Want to start your own businesses
   …and more.

WHY: Chronic unemployment is a human condition that can be as deadly in its far-reaching effects as a major illness. It is potentially anxiety producing, depressing, esteem deflating, and can produce a mental and spiritual state so deteriorated that the unemployed person may stop trying to find work, risking further deterioration. Worse, he or she may come to deny the usefulness of biblical teachings and/or the existence of a living, loving God. Once such a state takes root in the job seeker's psyche, he or she becomes far less likely to job search and, consequently, to press toward the mark of the high calling of God in Christ Jesus in accordance with Philippians 3:14.

Believing God for Work's mission is to minister scripturally sound support to you, job seeker, so that you may be better equipped to maintain your resolve to find a job and to remain confidently seated in your faith until you do. **This book's main tenets** are that:

- God reveals His will to us daily and it is our responsibility to prayerfully seek his will for every aspect of our lives including job seeking. Consider Ephesians 2:10: *For we are His workmanship, created in Christ Jesus unto good works, which God hath before ordained that we should walk in them.*

- Worksites are one of the best places for God to teach us how to hone and apply our gifts and talents to benefit others.

- If allowed to do so, God will faithfully develop us so that we can have a positive impact on the lives of those around us regardless of which occupations we are seated in.

- God has a purpose (or two!) for each of our lives. When we become determined to live godly lives, He assists us in finding employment, for instance, that best suits us so that we may be a benefit to others through the gifts and talents He placed within us.

My prayer for you, dear reader, is for God to bless any willingness on your part to take the Bible scriptures contained herein to heart so that you move thereby in the strength and power of their truths toward gainful employment.

3

May your gifts explode at your future worksite for the good of those you meet there, may your new employers become prosperous because of the godly character you exhibit at your new worksite, and may you <u>tenaciously</u> *believe God for work* until you are employed!

LeDene Lewis
Believe.Godforwork@sbcglobal.net

Part 2

Believing God for Work

God worked from the very beginning (Genesis 1:1), and according to other scriptures also recorded in Genesis, He even admired his work —seeing that it was good.

Further, God was the first employer, assigning the vocation of gardener to Adam prior to the Fall (Genesis 2:15). God's Son was a carpenter. The apostle Paul was a tentmaker.

It seems safe to say, then, that work in and of itself is a good thing and is an activity endorsed by God for us.

I wonder why it is, then, that so many people whom I have coached during my 20-plus years in workforce development, people who say they believe in God, have been reluctant to pray to God *specifically* for employment (or any other specific need for that matter). It surprises me to this day how many people say that they don't want to "bother" God with such a minuscule matter (meaning by comparison with all the other needs He is "busy" with) as their need for gainful employment, even though God clearly indicates in the scriptures that He cares about *everything* that has to do with us. Indeed, 1 Peter 5:7 tells us to cast *all* of our care upon Him, for He cares for us. Do note that 1 Peter does *not* say that He cares for us *except* in the area of employment.

Moreover, there are those hesitant to pray for work because they assert that originally God never intended for us to work—that working, laboring, was instituted as a curse in response to disobedience. And so now, the reasoning goes, if we do win employment, it is our lot in life to suffer gladly through it. However, it is my opinion that it was the *ground* that was cursed—that is, work itself became hard (see Genesis 3:17-19); and that the *activity* of working always was a good and indeed a desirable thing. Consider Ecclesiastes 3:13, which says in part that every man should enjoy the good of all his work and that it is the *gift* of God.

All that being said, let me be careful to say that God does not mandate that people must work outside of their homes. Rather, God does see work and working –which usually is a result of employment—as a good thing and, therefore, answerable via prayers.

About the Scriptures Chosen for This Book

Power is in part defined as the authority, ability, and right to take a particular action or to accomplish a particular goal. S*criptures* (as defined for our purposes) are the sacred writings of the Christian religions, especially those expressed in bibles. So *power scriptures* can be said to be those scriptures that are particularly applicable for building faith to sustain us as we anticipate a successful outcome for some specific need —such as for a new job. This book is filled with hundreds of *power scriptures*. However, offered below are the book's foundational power scriptures.

Deuteronomy 29:9: Keep therefore the words of this covenant, and do them, that ye may prosper in all that ye do.

Psalm 35:27: Let them say continually, let the Lord be magnified, which hath pleasure in the prosperity of his servant.

Proverbs 3:5, 6: Trust in the Lord with all thine heart; and lean not unto thine own understanding. In all thy ways acknowledge Him, and He shall direct thy paths.

Ecclesiastes 5:19: Every man also to whom God hath given...power...to rejoice in his labor; this is the gift of God.

2 Timothy 3:16: All scripture is given by inspiration of God, and is profitable for doctrine, for reproof, for correction, for instruction in righteousness.

1 John 5:14, 15: And this is the confidence that we have in Him, that, if we ask anything according to His will, He heareth us: And if we know that He hear us, whatsoever we ask, we know that we have the petitions that we desired of Him.

With faith set as flint, please use these and the other scriptures contained herein to *believe God for work.*

Section 2:
Powering Up for Work

Part 1

Seven Possible Reasons for Prolonged Unemployment

First John 5:14,15 tells us: *And this is the confidence that we have in Him, that if we ask any thing according to His will, He heareth us: And if we know that He hear us, whatsoever we ask, we know that we have the petitions that we desired of Him.*

For those of you who have experienced a lengthy job search process, this scripture begs the question, why then is it taking so long to find a new job? Spiritually put, the question becomes, What may cause a prayer for a godly thing to go unanswered?

The more superficial (but nevertheless true) reasons for prolonged unemployment can be found in almost any newspaper. For instance, some articles blame economic twists and downturns; others blame a lack of governmental funding to meet needs of social services and/or jobs programs. However, have you ever noticed that there are people who, despite facing the same so-called negative economic conditions as everyone else, still manage to find employment relatively quickly? Could it be that there are other considerations besides those listed above? I submit that there very well may be.

First John 3:21 tells us: *Beloved, if our hearts condemn us not, then have we confidence toward God.* When we pray for jobs (or for anything else for that matter), we will need to have confidence toward God that He will answer us. Offered here for your prayerful consideration are seven possible reasons why we may begin to doubt whether God will answer our prayers—reasons why the job search may be prolonged.

Haggai 1:5
Now therefore thus saith the Lord of hosts:
Consider your ways.

Possible Reason **#1** for Prolonged Unemployment: Being a Trap for Resources Instead of a Funnel

This first reason for prolonged unemployment has to do with any unwillingness on our part to allow God to use what He has given to us for others' benefit. For example, we know that working usually yields a paycheck. So the question to consider is how willing were we to share a portion of our income (and/or other resources, such as our time, experience, etc.) when last employed?

If we understand that nothing we have has a personal significance to a Being who created the universe and owns everything that is in it, we can then realize that God does not personally need anything we have—including our money. What He desires is our willingness to share our resources so that others may be won to Him, for instance, and/or to be developed in His ways. That means that what we possess has its greatest significance in its ability to be used to meet the needs of others through our willingness to share.

What's wonderful and reassuring is that all along, throughout our willingness to give, He meets our own needs. Look at Deuteronomy 8:18: *But thou shalt remember the*

Lord thy God: For it is He that giveth thee power to get wealth, <u>that He may establish His covenant</u>.
Further, by sharing what God has given to us, we are giving to *Him*. Look at Matthew 25:37-40: Then *shall the righteous answer Him, saying, Lord, when saw we thee and hungered, and fed thee? or thirsty, and gave thee drink?... and took thee in... and clothed thee?...Or saw thee... in prison, and came unto thee? ...*[and the Lord answered] *Inasmuch as ye have done it unto one of the least of these my brethren, ye have done it unto Me.*

**Have you been a trap for money
or any other resource instead of being a funnel?**

<u>Possible Reason **#2** for Prolonged Unemployment:</u>
Being an Unjust Leader

It is possible that sometimes we can suffer protracted unemployment because of an unwillingness to repent for how we have handled ourselves in leadership roles in our previous jobs. For instance, when you were last a workplace leader, did you cheat (or otherwise slight) someone out of his or her wages in some way? Malachi 3:5 tells us: *And I will come near to you to judgment; and I will be a swift witness against the sorcerers, and against the adulterers, and against false swearers, and against those that oppress the hireling in his wages.* Notice that God holds those who defraud laborers of their wages just as subject to receiving His judgment as He does sorcerers, adulterers, and liars.
Or did you ever "get even" with a staff person during his performance appraisal by using the appraisal form as a

11

tool to retaliate for some personal matter you had against him? Or perhaps you yielded to the temptation to steal ideas from others by claiming that they were your own. Did you ever falsify your time sheet and/or allow others to do so?

Second Samuel 23:3 says that *He that ruleth over men must be just, ruling in the fear of God.* To rule in the fear of God doesn't mean we follow His ways because we are afraid that He is just waiting to bop us on the head if we get out of line. Rather, it means we should lead others with a reverential respect of God and of His ways of doing things. After all, it was God who gave us favor with our bosses to promote us to leadership roles in the first place.

If you abused your authority in a former position, have you apologized to God?

Possible Reason #3 for Prolonged Unemployment:
Living Contrary to Christ-Like Standards

The third possible reason for prolonged unemployment deals mostly with our character—with how we as Christians behaved at our previous worksites. But the principle here is true for all job seekers who claim to believe in God. Questions to ask include: Did we "borrow" company supplies for personal use? Did we get in cahoots with doctors to extend our sick time from work or have a doctor forge our worker's compensation claims when we were perfectly healthy? Or did we habitually backbite authority figures and co-workers or otherwise defame their characters against

12

the teaching of Leviticus 19:16: Thou *shalt not go up and down as a talebearer among thy people...*?

What kinds of un-Christ-like behaviors did you engage in when you were last employed? If you have never been employed, then consider how you now behave around your family and friends as an unemployed person. Are you mean to them?

You could argue (and you would win) that no one is perfect. We all have missed opportunities to please God at one time or another. But what's important is what we did after we discovered that we had offended Him through, for instance, the mistreatment of others.

Put another way, would *you* continue to provide something for someone if he or she consistently mistreated it? Likewise, if we insist on being a poor steward of the jobs He provides for us—wreaking havoc where we are planted—why should he provide us with yet another job so that we can continue to hurt even more people? We would do well to take heed of Psalm 84:11: *For the Lord God is a sun and shield...no good thing will He withhold from them that walk uprightly.*

Did your former workplace behaviors betray your spiritual code of conduct?

Possible Reason **#4** for Prolonged Unemployment:
Having Faith Without Corresponding Actions

What good is it to believe that God will provide us with new jobs if we don't involve ourselves in the kinds of activities a successful job search requires? Engaging in unfocused, nonproductive avoidance-type activities is the fourth possible reason for prolonged unemployment.

Regardless of the fact that He is able to do so, God is not likely to open our ceilings with some huge can opener and drop employers down into our living rooms. We are told in James 2:14 that *faith without works* [activities which demonstrate that we expect our faith to be answered] *is dead* [nonproductive]. That means we can pray for a new job for hours on end, but if we won't update our resumes; won't complete job applications; won't practice interviewing; and won't seek out employers, then there is nothing to serve as a base upon which the favor of God can rest on our behalf to bring us the jobs we say we want. Perhaps we could do volunteer work for employers in order to get on board at desired companies. Perhaps we could take a few classes to update our skills. If any of you have a criminal record and need to gather reference letters, have you done so?

The point is that action is required to mix with our faith in order to acquire a new job. James 2:18 says in part: *I will show Thee my faith by my works.* And James 2:20 reiterates the point: *But wilt thou know, O vain man, that faith without works is dead?*

Do you dream of having a new job but are not certain which "works" to undertake to make it happen? Pray Psalm 25:4, 5a: *Show me Thy ways, O Lord; teach me Thy paths. Lead me in Thy truth, and teach me.*

Do your activities demonstrate your belief that you will find employment?

Possible Reason **#5** for Prolonged Unemployment:
Asking for Employment Amiss

The fifth possible reason for prolonged unemployment has to do with our hearts' motives for wanting work. James 4:3 tells us: Ye *ask, and receive not because ye ask amiss, that ye may consume it upon your lusts.* We ask for employment amiss when the reason we want a particular job is because we covet the prestige a particular title accords, for instance. Or perhaps we become so focused on how much salary the position pays that we don't allow ourselves to be guided by God regarding His choice of occupation for us. How will we sense His leading if prestige, money, or other distractions have captured all of our prayer time?   Consider Matthew 6:31-33: *Therefore take no thought...for your heavenly Father knoweth that ye have need of all these things. But seek ye first the kingdom of God, and his righteousness; and all these things shall be added unto you.*

We are asked as believers to consider *first* His plan for our lives--trusting him to see to it that eventually we will end up precisely where He needs us to be. Indeed, John 9:31 tells us: *...if any man be a worshipper of God, and doeth His will, him He heareth.* And it is according to His will that we are to be seated in jobs that would take the most advantage of our talents, skills, personalities, and gifts. Let us be about the business of praying for *those* kinds of jobs.

What is your heart's motive for seeking the kinds of jobs you seek?

15

Possible Reason **#6** for Prolonged Unemployment:
Being Ashamed of Small Beginnings

I wonder what would have happened to little Maggie Lena Walker (1867-1934) had she decided as a young girl that being born to a poor washerwoman meant her fate was sealed—that she was destined to follow the same poverty-bound track as her mother? My guess is that she, an African American growing up in Richmond, Virginia, in 1800's America, never would have been the first American woman to found a bank: the Saint Luke Penny Savings Bank, in 1903 in Richmond, Virginia.

Scripture puts it this way in the book of Job 8:7: *Though thy beginning was small, yet thy latter end should greatly increase.* But if we do nothing to affect our latter end, it will remain as meager as any meager beginning. For instance, if an opportunity comes that requires us to enter a company at a level or two lower than our pride would rather, let us decide that through our diligence and quality of productivity we will eventually succeed up and out of our "small beginnings." And while it's true that every job does not offer a career track leading from less to greater responsibility and a higher income, it is also true that every job does offer experience. The beauty of experience is that it can be gathered from—and carried to—successive employers.

**Have you allowed your pride
to talk you out of accepting a "small-beginnings" job
despite an "inward leading" to accept?**

Possible Reason #7 for Prolonged Unemployment:
Ignoring the Call to Reconcile

There are times when we stroll down paths not lighted by God's word, embarking upon avenues not of God's design for our lives. For instance, in the workplace we may have become traps for resources God has blessed us with instead of caring, sharing funnels. Or perhaps we treated people poorly, especially those who looked to us for leadership. Maybe others of us strolled down the path of the workaholic and hurt our families by ignoring them as we pursued more money and more prestige. Maybe we became embroiled in an office romance with a married person or with a single person while married.

Whether your particular path of error is listed above or not, take time in prayer to ask to have revealed to you that consistent misstep that may have caused you to feel less connected to God. Whatever it was, if you remain impenitent, you run the risk of leading yourself away from God's ways and wisdom—not a good place to be. Consider 2 Corinthians 5:20: ...*we pray you in Christ's stead, be ye reconciled to God.* That prayer of Paul the Apostle calls for people to bring themselves from a state of disagreement back into unity with God. It is a prayer most fitting to pray for ourselves.

The good news is in 1 John 1:9: *If we confess our sins, He is faithful and just to forgive us our sins, and to cleanse us from all unrighteousness.* Once cleansed, we are free to rejoin Him on the correct path for our life. And then our heart won't betray our faith when we pray for a new job.

Have you been ignoring God's call to reconcile with Him?

Part 2

Ten Commandments for a Successful Job Search

The *Ten Commandments* in the Bible is not merely a listing of God's do's and don'ts for our lives. It is a code of wise conduct, a peace-sustaining mode of operating, which was given to us so that we may live efficiently and effectively within God's will for our lives.

Modeled after the book of Exodus' style of presenting principles for successful living, offered here are ten commandments for a successful job search. These too are not merely do's and don'ts but are tried-and-true pieces of advice validated through my more than 20 years' experience in workforce development. They are offered to provide fuel for thought for prayerful self-examination, and they are as biblically sound as I was able to interpret application for our subject matter of job searching.

Commandment #1 for a Successful Job Search: Consider Your Ways

Haggai 1:6, 7
...he that earneth wages earneth wages to put it into
a bag with holes.
Thus saith the Lord of hosts; Consider your ways.

In Section I you were asked to take a look at seven possible reasons for prolonged unemployment. If after reading through the seven reasons, you discover that there are things in your past for which you need to ask God for forgiveness, let me encourage you to tackle those things now and get yourself reattached to (back in fellowship with) God. After doing so, it is important to commit yourself to monitoring your lifestyle so that you are able to consistently demonstrate your commitment to your Christian—or most ideal—principles.

A good way for us to maintain a renewed commitment to developing a closer walk with God is for us to examine our actions daily and to strive to make any necessary adjustments as quickly as we can. Questions to ask ourselves include: Have I been especially unkind lately? Was I selfish or especially self-centered and unyielding about anything? Have I been gorging myself on all the wrong foods in fits of self-pity about being out of work, or have I been otherwise punishing my "temple" with alcohol, prescription medications, or illegal substances? A *yes* response to even one of those questions indicates that some changing needs to be done.

In these tough economic times with the job market so competitive, we most certainly need our faith to be rock-solid strong for believing in God for new jobs. Don't allow past unconfessed/unforgiven actions impede answers to prayers for employment.

When was the last time you examined mental footage of your day's behaviors?

Commandment #II for a Successful Job Search:
Let God Be Your Career Counselor

Jeremiah 10:23
**O Lord, I know that the way of man is not in himself:
it is not in man that walketh to direct his steps.**

Long before setting out on the quest for a new job, you must prayerfully ask, "Lord, which occupation do *You* want me to take?" This is not an exercise in religiosity. In fact, if we consider it to be true that He made us, then it makes perfect since that He just may know us more intimately than we know ourselves.

There are gifts and talents planted in us by God, which we are to use in our places of employment. Therefore, let's strive to be seated in jobs of His will, based on how He designed us. Consider Psalm 139:1-3: *O Lord, Thou hast searched me, and known me. Thou knowest my downsitting and mine uprising, thou understandest my thought afar off. Thou comprehend my path and my lying down, and art acquainted with all my ways.*

There may be times when you will want to seek the advice of a professional career counselor to help you navigate a junction or two between career choices. Indeed, we are advised in Proverbs 15:22: *Without counsel purposes are disappointed: but in the multitude of counselors they are established.* However, as faith-walking believers, we are to seek God's counsel *first* . Proverbs 28:5 tells us: *...they that seek the Lord understand all things.*

May your journey for a new job begin with prayerful consultation with God about which direction you should take in your job-searching efforts.

Psalm 32:8
I will instruct thee and teach thee in the way
which thou shalt go:
I will guide thee with Mine eye.

Commandment #III for a Successful Job Search:
Fear Not

Deuteronomy 31:8
And the Lord, He it is that doth go before thee;
He will be with thee,
He will not fail thee, neither forsake thee:
fear not, neither be dismayed.

What sort of things do job seekers fear? They may fear the interviewing process, or having to learn new skills, or not having what it takes to learn new skills. They may fear that they fall short of having the right experience, or that they don't have the "right" skin color or the desired height, gender, or age. They may fear that their criminal records will prevent anyone from ever wanting to hire them. In short, they fear, for whatever the reason, that they don't have what it takes to win new employment.

Added to that, they may fear that not having a job will lead to losing their homes, having their cars repossessed, being deserted by their significant others, being disrespected by their children due to an inability to provide for them, and

21

on and on goes the list—for fear can be a consuming fire.

Consider 2 Timothy 1:7: *For God hath not given us the spirit of fear; but of power, and of love, and of a sound mind.* Notice that it says in that power scripture that a spirit of fear does not come from God. So whenever we find ourselves filled with anxiety (fear's first cousin) about any component of the job-search process, we must not allow ourselves to be foiled by it.

Let us not focus on the skills we lack. Rather, let's focus on what we do have to offer and then boldly—that is, fearlessly—offer that to employers.

2 Corinthians 8:11,12
Now therefore perform the doing of it; that as there was a readiness to will,
so there may be a performance also out of that which
ye have.

Commandment **#IV** for a Successful Job Search:
Assemble Yourself with Believers

James 5:16
Pray one for another, that ye may be healed.

Do you remember when the concept of synergy was all the rage? Very basically, a synergetic relationship is said to be one in which the combined contribution of ideas and actions from a group of people produces more of an impact on outcomes than can the sum of each person's ideas and actions alone. Synergy is still a very popular business concept today and is used widely for achieving desired outcomes.

Spiritually speaking then, the concept of synergy can be adapted here to mean that where there are two or more people in agreement in prayer, there is more force available for accomplishing goals than when each person stands alone. Consider Matthew 18:19: *I say unto you, that if two of you shall agree on earth as touching any thing that they shall ask, it shall be done for them of my Father which is in heaven.* And Hebrews 10:23 and 25: *Let us hold fast the profession of our faith without wavering;* (for he is faithful that promised) *not forsaking the assembling of ourselves together...but exhorting one another.*

Why are we instructed in the book of Hebrews to come together? for the *support* we can gain from (and provide to) each other through a common system of beliefs and values.

Why may a job seeker need the support of other believers as he stands in faith for a new job—particularly if the job search process becomes protracted? Because there are serious negative side effects that can attach themselves to the unemployed (especially in the case of chronic unemployment) that include:

- Sense of hopelessness, with mental depression and/ or accompanying low self-esteem and frustration;

- Hypersensitivity to rejection (even in areas not related to job searching);

- Acts of desperation, including lying, stealing, cheating (most often out of fears surrounding lack of income);

23

- Acting-out behaviors that include inappropriate application of anger and hostility and inordinate touchiness and antisocial behaviors, as well as an insatiable need for attention;

- Mental fatigue, chronic physical illness (either from extreme self-neglect or gross overindulgence);

- Self-expulsion from and deterioration of positive relationships (a migration toward deprived relationships—"birds-of-a-feather" mentality for "support");

- Deterioration of job skills due to lack of use, which in turn acts as kindling for fueling negative self-esteem;

- Abuse of legal and illegal substances;

- Turning away from previously held spiritual beliefs and/or other positive support systems.

Let us not withdraw into ourselves thereby missing opportunities to strengthen—and to be strengthened by—others. Let's steep ourselves in the comfort of *can-do* thinkers, people who not only believe in what the scriptures have to say about their own eventual success but who also believe in *us*.

2 Corinthians 1:3,4
Blessed be...the God of all comfort;
Who comforteth us in all our tribulation,
that we may be able to comfort them which are in any trouble,
by the comfort wherewith we ourselves are comforted of God.

Commandment #V for a Successful Job Search:
Learn About Yourself Through Your Skills and Gifts

Proverbs 24:3-5
Through wisdom is an house builded; and by understanding it is established;
and by knowledge shall the chambers be filled with all precious and pleasant riches...
a man of knowledge increaseth strength.

Exercise your imagination for a moment and think of the job-search process, in particular, interviewing, as a stage production with its obligatory regimens for making ready for a successful performance. There are scripts to be studied (your resume and all other employment documents) and rehearsals to be attended (practicing your interviewing technique). A job seeker, like an actor, has to make ready in order to "wow" the audience—the potential employer.

The primary objective of your role as job candidate is to be a star—that is, you are to stand heads above the other applicants. You want interviewers to clamor for you to make a curtain call—a second interview. To accomplish that, you will have to know your lines about yourself *cold*. So well in fact, that if the interviewer "comes off script"— that is, asks you something a bit off the wall, such as *Why is green a great color?*—you will be ready.

Let's say you are applying for a sales position, and you already know from your time of self-study that you are a go-getter. In response to the why-green-is-a-great-color question, you might offer that green is like a "go" sign to you. You might go on to explain that the color symbolizes action—efficient movement to close deals successfully, for instance.

Come to so fine an understanding of what makes you productive *and* unproductive that you are easily able to skillfully express what you can contribute to a company. That can only happen if you take the time to learn about your working-self thoroughly.

Commandment #VI for a Successful Job Search:
Exploit the Power of Your Employment Documents

Habakkuk 2:2
And the Lord answered me, and said, Write the vision,
and make it plain upon tables, that he may run that readeth it.

When we exploit something, we act to manipulate it for our own good to gain an advantage. To gain an advantage when job searching, you will have to "manipulate" your resume, job applications, letters of reference, college transcripts, certificates of achievement, diplomas, and awards so that they become a united body of work, a volume that you could literally entitle, *Why I Would Make a Wise Hire.*

Our employment documents have the powerful potential to make or break hiring decisions since they tell of the good *and* the bad in our work histories. So, generally speaking, wise job seekers exploit their paperwork by digging deeply for any talent, accomplishment, experience, etc., inherent in their work (including unpaid experience). Wise job seekers bring all of the "goods" to the spotlight and unabashedly declare their worth. And they do so with consistency. That means the application does not contradict the resume, which does not contradict reference letters, etc. Understand that our employment documents must stand on their own merit since we may not always be there to explain to their readers the information contained in them.

Gain an advantage with employers by writing the "vision" of who you are so clearly that a compelling case is made for calling you in for an interview solely based on how you look on paper. Come to understand the importance of fully exploiting your employment documents.

Do all of your employment documents suggest that you would make a wise hire?

Commandment #VII for a Successful Job Search:
Seek Work Until You Find It

Jeremiah 29:11
For I know the thoughts that I think toward you, saith the Lord, thoughts of peace, and not of evil, to give you an *expected* end.

What if someone you trusted told you that if you searched long enough, that if you just kept at it, you would find a great treasure? How diligently would you search? More than likely you would search tirelessly, determined to stay your course until you found that treasure.

For a faith-walking job seeker who lives trusting God with every detail of his or her life no matter what, the job search can be likened to that of a treasure hunt. That is, the seeker can have a high degree of confidence that there really is a treasure—a job —for him out there *somewhere*. He can reason that when one employer turns him down, eventually another will want to hire him.

But how can a believer really *know* that he will eventually win employment? Such confidence stems from an understanding that God *wants* to give us good things. We established early on that God sees the activity of working as a good thing. So we know He endorses the activity as something worth desiring. Psalm 37:4 tells us that if we delight ourselves in the Lord, He shall give us the desires of our hearts.

Psalm 37:5 tells us that if we commit our way to Him and trust Him, He shall bring it to pass. What is our "it" in this case? A new job.

All things being equal (meaning you have a dedicated faith walk and trust Whom you believe), the day will come when you will find work. Visualize that expected end in faith at the very beginning of your job search, and hang on to that hope until your new job materializes.

Hebrews 10:35
Cast not away your confidence, which hath great recompense of reward.

Commandment #VIII for a Successful Job Search:
Don't Take Rejection to Heart

Proverbs 4:23
Keep thy heart with all diligence for out of it are the issues of life.

28

If you are building something and choose to use a hammer instead of a screwdriver, does that mean that you believe the screwdriver to be a bad thing or a thing to be avoided forever? Does your selection of the hammer mean that the screwdriver will never be useful to you again? Of course not. But some job seekers behave as if it's true that if an employer chooses another job candidate instead of them, they will be rejected by all employers Forever. And so they lose the heart to try.

A cause of disheartenment for job seekers is that they forget to keep—or guard, as the Bible puts it—their hearts when employers select someone else instead of them. They often dissolve into quivering balls of self-doubt about the very same skills for which they trumpeted their confidence during the interview. If we lack confidence in what we have to offer to employers, we will eventually come to lack the motivation needed to continue the job search. We will then find ourselves breaking not only the subject commandment but also Commandments III, *Fear Not*, and VII, *Seek Work Until You Find It* (see above).

Let us always remember that not being chosen for a job does not mean our skills are worthless to *all* employers. When we refuse to take not being selected (rejection) to heart, we help to maintain our courage and our faith to continue to job search.

Matthew 9:29
...according to your faith be it unto you.

Commandment #IX for a Successful Job Search:
Accept Honest Labor Only

Proverbs 16:8
Better is a little with righteousness
than great revenues without right.

If we participate in behaviors that cause the genuineness of our spiritual beliefs to come into question, we serve to destroy our credibility as believers through our own hypocrisy; and we weaken our own faith toward God for answered prayer. For example, if our families or friends see us augmenting our incomes by selling illegal substances, they would be less inclined to believe it when we say that ours is a God who is able to provide for us. Worse, we risk not having a clean heart toward God and may, therefore, risk having our prayers for a new job go unanswered.

Look at it this way: Let's say that a child you loved asked you for a bike so he could ride it to school. You agree to buy it for him. How would you feel if before you could fulfill that promise, he takes it upon himself to snatch a bike away from another kid because, well, after all, he had an immediate need to get to school on it? His actions wouldn't fly with you (I trust). And until you two come to terms about his actions, you and that child will no longer see eye-to-eye, so to speak. It could be said that you two will be out of fellowship with one another because of bad behavior. Likewise, dishonest labor breaks our fellowship with God because He wants righteous (consonant with God's will) children; and he wants them to bring no harm to others.

Let us honor the first commandment listed in this book, *Consider Your Ways,* by refusing to be tempted to dishonor God by participating in questionable activities for any reason.

1 Corinthians 10:13
There hath no temptation taken you but such as
is common to man:
but God is faithful, who will not suffer you to be
tempted above that ye are able;
but will with the temptation also make a way to escape,
that ye may be able to bear it.

Commandment #X for a Successful Job Search:
Share Your Resources with God

Malachi 3:8
Will a man rob God? Yet ye have robbed Me.
But ye say, wherein have we robbed Thee?
In tithes and offerings.

If we Christians ever wish to spark a heated debate, we can always ask folks for their opinions about tithing. So first, I offer the following scriptures to counter the most common objections to tithing; my opinion about the matter follows. Please prayerfully consider:

Deuteronomy 8:18: But thou shalt remember the Lord thy God: for it is He that giveth thee power to get wealth, that He may establish His covenant which He swore unto thy fathers, as it is this day.

Proverbs 3:9: Honor the Lord with thy substance, and with the first fruits of all thine increase.

2 Corinthians 9:6-8: But this I say, He which soweth sparingly shall reap also sparingly; and he which soweth bountifully shall reap also bountifully.

1 John 3:17, 18: But whoso hath this world's good, and seeth his brother have need, and shutteth up his bowels of compassion from him, how dwelleth the love of God in him? My little children, let us not love in word, neither in tongue; but in deed and in truth.

From what I can see in the power scriptures above, we demonstrate our trust in God to provide for us, as well as show Him our willingness to be obedient to His word, when we give away a portion of what we have been given.

Some may ask, what if we give and the money is used for something other than for what we intended? If those receiving our resources abuse our trust by how they disburse what we give (a common argument for abstaining from tithing), our giving is still counted unto *us* for uprightness in God's sight; and he will honor our giving by rewarding us based on our heart's intent when we gave. Bear in mind the words in 1 Samuel 16:7: *...for the Lord seeth not as man seeth; for man looketh on the outward appearance, but the Lord looketh on the heart.*

But to those who *misuse* those funds, that misuse is counted against *them* as errant. Consider Malachi 3:5: *And I will come near to you to judgment; and I will be a swift witness against the sorcerers, and against the adulterers, and against false swearers, and against those that oppress* [defraud, acquire deceitfully] *the hireling in his wages.*

So while we want to be wise by giving where there is potential for spiritual fruit, let us not ignore, under the guise of "protecting" our money, all those scriptures above that encourage investing in our places of worship. Let's allow God to "protect" our money and provide for us in return for our faithfulness. Consider Luke 6:38: *Give, and it shall be given unto you; good measure, pressed down, and shaken together, and running over, shall men give into your bosom. For with the same measure that ye mete withal it shall be measured to you again.* And let us understand that we could never out-give God.

<u>Malachi 3:10</u>
Bring ye all the tithes into the storehouse,
that there may be meat in Mine house,
and prove Me now herewith, saith the Lord of hosts,
if I will not open you the windows of heaven,
and pour you out a blessing, that there shall not be room
enough to receive it.

Section 3:

Success Strategies
and
Corresponding Power Scriptures

WHEN YOU HAVE NEVER BEEN EMPLOYED

It is a voice of fear that says to us that since we have never been employed, then we have no hire-worthy experience and, therefore, we are not employable. Buying into that irrational supposition is a lot like concluding that if we have never ridden a bike, we are not able to ride one because, well, after all, we have never ridden one.

When job searching, the question we often ask ourselves is whether we have enough experience to be hired when a better first-question may be, How much do we *value* the experience we *do* have? Part of what convinces people who have never gotten a job that they won't get one is that they tend not to see their past work experiences (or volunteer work, etc.) as hire-worthy. But those who see value in *all* experience (whether paid or unpaid) will be better able to convey that value to employers. Consider Second Corinthians 8:12: *For if there be first a willing mind, it is accepted according to that a man hath, and not according to that he hath not.*

Let's say, for instance, that the job you applied for requires you to operate a particular type of machine. While you know that you do not have experience with that particular machine, you also know that you have had experience with a variety of machinery and that you are, in fact, mechanically inclined. So in this instance, you would confidently state during your interview that you expect to catch on quickly to how the machine works because you have a demonstrated knack for understanding mechanized things —as opposed to offering a negative statement such as, I don't know how to work the machine.

By putting our "haves" to work for us, we can minimize our fears and interview effectively; and that is true even when we have never worked before or are applying for jobs with tasks attached to them that are a bit foreign to us.

Power Scriptures for *When You Have Never Been Employed*

Deuteronomy 31: 6: Be strong and of a good courage, fear not, nor be afraid of them: for the Lord thy God, He it is that doth go with thee; He will not fail thee, nor forsake thee.

2 Chronicles 20:20: Believe in the Lord your God, so shall ye be established...so shall ye prosper.

Job 36:11: If they obey and serve Him, they shall spend their days in prosperity, and their years in pleasures.

Psalm 121:2: My help cometh from the Lord, which made heaven and earth.

Psalm 118:25: Save now, I beseech Thee, O Lord: O Lord, I beseech Thee, send now prosperity.

Proverbs 8:21: That I may cause those that love me to inherit substance; and I will fill their treasures.

Ecclesiastes 7:8: Better is the end of a thing than the beginning thereof; and the patient in spirit is better than the proud in spirit.

Isaiah 41:13: For I the Lord thy God will hold thy right hand, saying unto thee, Fear not; I will help thee.

Jeremiah 32:17: Ah Lord God! behold, Thou hast made the heaven and the earth by Thy great power and stretched out arm, and there is nothing too hard for Thee.

Romans: 8:32: He that spared not His own Son, but delivered Him up for us all, how shall he not with Him also freely give us all things?

Ephesians 6:10: Finally, my brethren, be strong in the Lord, and in the power of His might.

Philippians 4:13: I can do all things through Christ which strengtheneth me.

2 Timothy 2:1: Thou therefore, My son, be strong in the grace that is in Christ Jesus.

1 John 2:27: But the anointing which ye have received of Him abideth in you, and ye need not that any man teach you: but as the same anointing teacheth you of all things, and is truth, and is no lie, and even as it hath taught you, ye shall abide in Him.

WHEN YOUR JOB LOSS WAS DUE TO THE ACTIONS OF OTHERS

When jobs are lost due to the actions of a workplace enemy or an unjust leader, or if our companies move away from us, or if we are cut from the rolls due to a layoff—then we know that the job loss was not within our control, not our fault. Being faultless, particularly when we have fallen prey to unjust actions of others, is kindling for fueling bitterness. And unless we arrest any bitterness toward others (or toward our former places of employment) at the root, the negative thoughts about these events could have us in a stranglehold of bitterness. And strangleholds have a way of causing us to become mentally and physically stagnant, which is a deadly state to be in when searching for a job.

How can we tell if bitterness is settling into our psyches? If, for instance, we are biting off the heads of our family members or are gruff to strangers for no apparent reason, then chances are high that we may be in the throes of bitterness.

Instead, forgive former co-workers, bosses, and all others for any part they played in your losing your job, and move on. Notice, I didn't just say to move on. That is because moving on without forgiveness produces as strong a stranglehold as does bitterness.

Not relishing the idea of forgiving those who have treated you unjustly? Perhaps this will help: We are not forgiving them *for them*. We are forgiving them because **a)** God said to ―so in essence we are doing it *for Him*; **b)** our forgiving them opens the door for God to forgive *us* when we mess up; and **c)** all the wrath we can muster while storming around our homes will not change our circumstances for the better one iota.

But our misplaced wrath *will* hurt and alienate those we may need the most. Let us forgive, forget, and move on.

Power Scriptures for *When Your Job Loss Was Due to the Actions of Others*

Proverbs 19:11: The discretion of a man deferreth his anger; and it is his glory to pass over a transgression.

Psalm 9:15, 16: The heathen are sunk down in the pit that they made, in the net which they hid is their own foot taken. The Lord is known by the judgment which He executeth: the wicked is snared in the work of his own hands.

Psalm 27:12: Deliver me not over unto the will of mine enemies: for false witnesses are risen up against me, and such as breathe out cruelty.

Psalm 41:11: By this I know that Thou favorest me, because mine enemy doth not triumph over me.

Psalm 55:18: He hath delivered my soul in peace from the battle that was against me: for there were many with me.

Psalm 94:21-23: They gather themselves together against the soul of the righteous, and condemn the innocent blood. But the Lord is my defense; and my God is the rock of my refuge. And He shall bring upon them their own iniquity, and shall cut them off in their own wickedness; yea, the Lord our God shall cut them off.

Psalm 141:10: Let the wicked fall into their own nets, whilst that I withal escape.

Matthew 5:44: But I say unto you, Love your enemies, bless them that curse you, do good to them that hate you, and pray for them which despitefully use you, and persecute you.

Romans 12:19: Dearly beloved, avenge not yourselves, but rather give place unto wrath: for it is written, Vengeance is Mine; I will repay, saith the Lord.

2 Thessalonians 1:4-6: So that we ourselves glory in You in the churches of God for Your patience and faith in all Your persecutions and tribulations that Ye endure: seeing it is a righteous thing with God to recompense tribulation to them that trouble you.

2 Thessalonians 3:16: Now the Lord of peace Himself give you peace always by all means. The Lord be with you all.

1 Peter 3:13, 14, 16: And who is he that will harm you, if ye be followers of that which is good? But and if ye suffer for righteousness' sake, happy are ye: and be not afraid of their terror, neither be troubled; having a good conscience; that, whereas they speak evil of you, as of evildoers, they may be ashamed that falsely accuse your good conversation in Christ.

WHEN THE JOB LOSS WAS YOUR FAULT

For those of you who had a hand in the demise of your jobs, offered here is the same advice also offered to those whose job loss was *not* their faults: forgive, forget, and move on. While we may feel badly about an action of ours that cost us our jobs, we should remember that there is a difference between experiencing grief and being overtaken by it. The negative effects of the latter will bring job search activities to a screeching halt. Or perhaps we may still job search with some degree of fervor but may unwittingly present ourselves poorly to prospective employers due to a subconscious feeling of guilt about how the last job was lost.

For instance, whenever prospective employers ask in interviews about our previous employment, our shoulders may droop and our once-confident manner of speaking may turn into barely audible mumblings, as we sadly (or angrily) recount our separation events --not a pretty sight to interviewers.

If you are carrying guilt around about how you separated from your last job, it might help you to realize that it might not be how you separated from the last job that is scaring off prospective employers; it could be how you are presenting those events to them.

Finally, would God ask us to forgive others and yet have us beat ourselves up about our own misdoings? No. We are taught that if we confess our mistakes, God forgives and refreshes us. Are you carrying yourself as if you were forgiven and refreshed?

<u>Power Scriptures</u> for *When the Job Loss Was Your Fault*

Psalm 3:3: But thou, O Lord, art a shield for me; my Glory, and the lifter up of mine head.

Psalm 31:9: Have mercy upon me, O Lord, for I am in trouble: mine eye is consumed with grief, yea, my soul and my belly.

Psalm 103:12: As far as the east is from the west, so far hath He removed our transgressions from us.

Psalm 107:6: Then they cried unto the Lord in their trouble, and He delivered them out of their distresses.

Proverbs 15:13: A merry heart maketh a cheerful countenance: but by sorrow of the heart the spirit is broken.

Isaiah 51:11: Therefore the redeemed of the Lord shall return, and come with singing unto Zion; and everlasting joy shall be upon their head: they shall obtain gladness and joy; and sorrow and mourning shall flee away.

Daniel 9:9: To the Lord our God belong mercies and forgivenesses, though we have rebelled against Him.

Zechariah 9:13: Turn you to the strong hold, ye prisoners of hope: even today do I declare that I will render double unto thee.

1 John 1:9: If we confess our sins, He is faithful and just to forgive us [our] sins, and to cleanse us from all unrighteousness.

Romans 14:22: Hast thou faith? Have it to thyself before God. Happy is he that condemneth not himself in that thing which He alloweth.

2 Corinthians 1:3, 4: Blessed be God, even the Father of our Lord Jesus Christ, the Father of mercies, and the God of all comfort; Who comforteth us in all our tribulation, that we may be able to comfort them which are in any trouble, by the comfort wherewith we ourselves are comforted of God.

2 Corinthians 2:7: So that contrariwise ye ought rather to forgive him, and comfort him, lest perhaps such a one should be swallowed up with overmuch sorrow.

2 Thessalonians 2:16, 17: Now our Lord Jesus Christ Himself, and God, even our Father, which hath loved us, and hath given us everlasting consolation and good hope through grace, Comfort your hearts, and establish you in every good word and work.

WHEN YOU DON'T KNOW WHERE TO START

At a point in your life when you were ready to undertake a new task but were not quite sure where to begin, did someone ever advise you to just begin at the beginning? Did you wonder just where that was for you? When beginning the job search process, know that God is the beginning. Sit still before Him, and ask Him where to start. Why?

A person who builds cars knows what makes them hum down the highway and, conversely, what makes them choke or breakdown. When we want to know about our cars, we go to the owner's manual or to the auto mechanic.

Similarly, our Father knows what makes a good employment fit for the skills, gifts, and talents He planted inside of us, as well as what can stop us from being all He created us to be.

In response to our prayers, He may direct us to take certain jobs and to avoid others; to seek the counsel of a career specialist, counselor, or an agency; or to attend school in order to sharpen our skills. But our doing any of those things should be preceded by seeking God's will and then taking action —and not the other way around.

Power Scriptures for *When You Don't Know Where to Start*

Psalm 16:11: Thou wilt show me the path of life: in Thy presence is fulness of joy; at Thy right hand there are pleasures for evermore.

Psalm 17:5: Hold up my goings in Thy paths, that my footsteps slip not.

Psalm 25:4: Show me Thy ways, O Lord; teach me Thy paths.

Psalm 25:9: The meek [teachable] will He guide in judgment: and the meek will He teach His way.

Psalm 37:23: The steps of a good man are ordered by the Lord and He delighteth in His way.

Psalm 48:14: For this is our God for ever and ever: He will be our guide even unto death.

Psalm 143:10: Teach me to do Thy will; for Thou art my God: Thy spirit is good; lead me into the land of uprightness.

Proverbs 3:6: In all Thy ways acknowledge Him, and He shall direct thy paths.

Proverbs 4:18: But the path of the just is as the shining light, that shineth more and more unto the perfect day.

Isaiah 48:17: Thus saith the Lord, Thy Redeemer, the Holy One of Israel; I am the Lord thy God which teacheth thee to profit, which leadeth thee by the way that thou shouldest go.

Matthew 6:33: But seek ye first the kingdom of God, and His righteousness; and all these things shall be added unto you.

Romans 11:29: For the gifts and calling of God are without repentance.

Philippians 4:6: Be anxious for nothing, but in everything by prayer and supplication, with thanksgiving, let your requests be made known to God.

2 Timothy 1:9: Who hath saved us, and called us with a holy calling, not according to our works, but according to His own purpose and grace, which was given us in Christ Jesus before the world began.

James 1:5: If any of you lack wisdom, let him ask of God, that giveth to all men liberally, and upbraideth not; and it shall be given him.

WHEN YOU FEEL LIKE LASHING OUT OR ARE OTHERWISE ANGRY

Some people lash out at others unprovoked when they lose what they consider to be their primary sources of security —their jobs. When we forget that God is the primary source for our needs, we lack the faith-sustaining revelation of the awesome provision made for us in Isaiah 48:17:

*I am the Lord thy God which teaches thee to profit, which
leads thee by the way you should go.* So in believing that
we are sinking, our fear may cause us to lash out, or
otherwise push others out of our lives, thereby alienating
people we love at a time we need them the most.

Let us never forget that there is no organization for
which we can work that will ever replace the Chief Source
for our needs. Rather, employers will always be mere
agents, our tools, through which our needs are provided
for. Therefore, as we do all of the practical activities for
securing employment, we must also trust God to provide
for us, thereby allowing peace to rule in our hearts. We will
then be better able to behave with civility toward others,
and that will be true despite how others act toward us.

So let us encourage peace within our families and
among our friends so that our prayers (including those for
new jobs) are not hindered due to the hardness of our hearts
toward others.

Power Scriptures for *When You Feel Like Lashing Out or Are Otherwise Angry*

Psalm 3:1, 3: Lord, how are they increased that
trouble me! Many are they that rise up against me. But
Thou, O Lord, art a shield for me; my Glory, and the lifter
up of mine head.

Proverbs 16:32: He that is slow to anger is better
than the mighty; and he that ruleth his spirit than he that
taketh a city.

Isaiah 61:7: For your shame ye shall have double.

Galatians 6:9: And let us not be weary in well doing:
for in due season we shall reap, if we faint not.

Ephesians 4:32: And be ye kind one to another, tenderhearted, forgiving one another, even as God for Christ's sake hath forgiven you.

Colossians 3:18, 19, 21: Wives, submit yourselves unto your own husbands, as it is fit in the Lord. Husbands, love your wives, and be not bitter against them. Fathers, provoke not your children to anger, lest they be discouraged.

Hebrews 12:14, 15: Follow peace with all men, and holiness, without which no man shall see the Lord: Looking diligently lest any man fail of the grace of God; lest any root of bitterness springing up trouble you, and thereby many be defiled.

James 1:20: For the wrath of man worketh not the righteousness of God.

1 Peter 3:7: Likewise, ye husbands, dwell with them according to knowledge, giving honor unto the wife…that your prayers be not hindered.

WHEN YOU NEED ENCOURAGEMENT

When we are feeling encouraged to accomplish, we tend to demonstrate a sense of hope for success, which shines on through to our actions. In contrast, when discouraged, we tend to behave just the opposite—as if we were depleted of power, down and out. That latter state of mind often happens to job seekers who experience a hope-depletion mixture of tiredness and frustration. They have lost the joy they had when they had hope of achieving success. They would do well to consider the words in Nehemiah 8:10: Then *he said…neither be ye sorry; for the joy of the Lord is your strength.*

How do we stir up and maintain our joy—our strength —in times as difficult as being unemployed? **a)** We thank and praise God for how He brought about our past successes; **b)** We thank Him that He is trustworthy to attend to our futures —even from the time of our conceptions. Psalm 139:13 tells us: *For Thou hast possessed my reins: Thou hast covered me in my mother's womb*; and **c)** We come to fully understand the implication of Psalm 35:27: *Let them shout for joy, and be glad, that favor my righteous cause; yea, let them say continually, Let the Lord be magnified, which hath pleasure in the prosperity of His servant.*

Take heart in knowing that you are in good hands.

Power Scriptures for *When You Need Encouragement*

Deuteronomy 31:6, 8: Be strong and of good courage, fear not, nor be afraid of them: for the Lord thy God, He it is that doth go with thee; He will not fail thee, nor forsake thee. And the Lord, He it is that doth go before thee; He will be with thee, He will not fail thee, neither forsake thee: fear not, neither be dismayed.

Psalm 27:13, 14: I had fainted, unless I had believed to see the goodness of the Lord in the land of the living. Wait on the Lord: be of good courage, and He shall strengthen thine heart: wait, I say, on the Lord.

Psalm 28:6: Blessed be the Lord, because He hath heard the voice of my supplications.

Psalm 34:18: The Lord is nigh unto them that are of a broken heart; and saveth such as be of a contrite spirit.

Psalm 29:1: The Lord will give strength unto His people; the Lord will bless His people with peace.

Psalm 37:4, 5: Delight thyself also in the Lord: and He shall give thee the desires of thine heart. Commit thy way unto the Lord; trust also in Him; and He shall bring it to pass.

Psalm 73:26: My flesh and my heart faileth: but God is the strength of my heart, and my portion for ever.

Matthew 11:28: Come unto Me, all ye that labor and are heavy laden, and I will give you rest.

1 Corinthians 2:9: But as it is written, eye hath not seen, nor ear heard, neither have entered into the heart of man, the things which God hath prepared for them that love Him.

Hebrews 13:5: Let your conversation be without covetousness; and be content with such things as ye have: for He hath said, I will never leave thee, nor forsake thee.

1 John 3:21: Beloved, if our heart condemn us not, then have we confidence toward God.

1 John 5:14, 15: And this is the confidence that we have in Him, that, if we ask any thing according to His will, He heareth us: And if we know that He hear us, whatsoever we ask, we know that we have the petitions that we desired of Him.

Galatians 6:9: And let us not be weary in well doing: for in due season we shall reap, if we faint not.

Philippians 4:6: Be anxious for nothing, but in everything by prayer and supplication, with thanksgiving, let your requests be made known to God.

WHEN FIGHTING FEARS ABOUT THE JOB SEARCH PROCESS IN GENERAL

Generally speaking, when we experience strong fears about job searching, it would do us well to explore whether those fears are *instinctive* or *intentional.* Instinctive fears are for the most part involuntary and are not necessarily bad. Experiencing instinctive fear of, say, a wild animal or a speeding car barreling down on us, may save our lives –as long as we are not paralyzed by the fear. Contrarily, there are *intentional* fears. These are not innate; rather, they are cultivated and strengthened by a well-fed negative thought life that says, for instance, that we will not attract employers.

Both instinctive and intentional fears can act as paralyzing agents, for as the mind and heart go, so goes the rest of the body. That means that if we have allowed our heads to decide that we will *never* find another job or that we will *never* earn enough money, etc., then we will also reason that the effort it takes to job search is pointless, and we will be more likely to give up job searching altogether.

When thoughts come to our minds that deny what scriptures say about our ability to become successful, we have to arrest their crippling potential by persistently reinforcing what the Word of God says. For instance, if we start to think that we will never again find work, we can counter that with Isaiah 43:19: *Behold, I will do a new thing; now it shall spring forth; shall ye not know it? I will even make a way in the wilderness, and rivers in the desert.*

We will have to consistently counter the negative effects of intentional fears with scriptural truths. Consider Corinthians 10:5: Casting *down imaginations, and every high thing that exalteth itself against the knowledge of God, and bringing into captivity every thought to the obedience of Christ.*

49

Power Scriptures for *When Fighting Fears About the Job Search Process in General*

Deuteronomy 1:12: Behold, the Lord thy God hath set the land before thee: go up and possess it, as the Lord God of thy fathers hath said unto thee; fear not, neither be discouraged.

Deuteronomy 31:8: And the Lord, He it is that doth go before thee; He will be with thee, He will not fail thee, neither forsake thee: fear not, neither be dismayed.

Psalm 34:4: I sought the Lord, and He heard me, and delivered me from all my fears.

Proverbs 29:25: The fear of man bringeth a snare: but whoso putteth his trust in the Lord shall be safe.

Psalm 118:6: The Lord is on my side; I will not fear: what can man do unto me?

Isaiah 26:3: Thou wilt keep him in perfect peace, whose mind is stayed on Thee: because he trusteth in Thee.

Isaiah 35:4: Say to them that are of a fearful heart, Be strong, fear not: behold, your God will come with vengeance, even God with a recompense; He will come and save you.

Isaiah 41:10: Fear thou not; for I am with thee: be not dismayed; for I am thy God: I will strengthen thee; yea, I will help thee; yea, I will uphold thee with the right hand of my righteousness.

Isaiah 44:8: Fear ye not, neither be afraid: have not I told thee from that time, and have declared it? Ye are even My witnesses. Is there a God beside me? Yea, there is no God; I know not any.

Luke 12:6, 7: Are not five sparrows sold for two farthings, and not one of them is forgotten before God? But even the very hairs of your head are all numbered. Fear not therefore: ye are of more value than many sparrows.

Romans 8:14, **15:** For as many as are led by the Spirit of God, they are the sons of God. For ye have not received the spirit of bondage again to fear; but ye have received the Spirit of adoption, whereby we cry, Abba, Father.

2 Timothy 1:7: For God hath not given us the spirit of fear; but of power, and of love, and of a sound mind.

WHEN YOU HAVE A CRIMINAL PAST

Psalm 142:7
Bring my soul out of prison, that I may praise Thy name: the righteous shall compass me about; for Thou shalt deal bountifully with me.

If you have a criminal past, you may find that there will be those who will treat you as if your past behavior is who you presently are and who you will be forever.
In other words, your challenge may be greater when others insist on applying negative labels to you due to your criminal past rather than to the criminal past itself —for ours is a society of labelers.

To disarm any potential power of negative labeling without lying about your past or becoming aggressive or defensive or deflated, you must see your own past as a closed concern despite attempts by others to reopen it or bring it forward into the now.

When you act in an interview as if the criminal behavior was something you *did* but no longer do, you will have an interviewing mindset that is difficult to puncture by even the most gifted of labelers

Continue to maintain your self-esteem and conviction of being the *changed* you, even if the employer tries to label you as an "ex-con" or an "ex-felon." For instance,

> **Employer:** *I see on your application that you are an ex-felon.*
>
> **You:** (calmly, confidently) *And "ex" to me means just that —something former. That is, I am now separated from the need to problem solve negatively, and instead offer strategic planning skills as well as….* Then continue taking the discussion forward by naming your skills and/or strengths.

Always allow the confidence of who you are *now* to speak to the employer much louder than the criminal behavior of your past. Refuse to live incarcerated behind others' bars of restraining and negative labels.

Power Scriptures for *When You Have a Criminal Past*

Numbers 13:33: And there we saw the giants…: and we were *in our own sight* as grasshoppers, and so we were *in their sight.*

Psalm 51:14: Deliver me from blood guiltiness, O God, thou God of my salvation: and my tongue shall sing aloud of Thy righteousness.

Psalm 69:16: Hear me, O Lord; for thy loving kindness is good: turn unto me according to the multitude of Thy tender mercies.

Psalm 71:20: Thou, which hast showed me great and sore troubles, shalt quicken me again, and shalt bring me up again from the depths of the earth.

Proverbs 28:13: He that covereth his sins shall not prosper: but whoso confesseth and forsaketh them shall have mercy.

Isaiah 42:6, 7: I the Lord have called thee in righteousness, and will hold thine hand, and will keep thee, and give thee for a covenant of the people, for a light of the Gentiles; to open the blind eyes, to bring out the prisoners from the prison, and them that sit in darkness out of the prison house.

Isaiah 43:25: I, even I, am He that blotteth out thy transgressions for Mine own sake, and will not remember thy sins.

Isaiah 61:7: For your shame ye shall have double; and for confusion they shall rejoice in their portion: therefore in their land they shall possess the double: everlasting joy shall be unto them.

Psalm 147:11: The Lord taketh pleasure in them that fear Him, in those that hope in His mercy.

Zechariah 9:12: Turn you to the stronghold, ye prisoners of hope: even today do I declare that I will render double unto thee.

Acts 5:25: Then came one and told them, saying, Behold, the men whom ye put in prison are standing in the temple, and teaching the people.

Romans 6:21, 22: What fruit had ye then in those things whereof ye are now ashamed? for the end of those things is death. But now being made free from sin, and become servants to God, ye have your fruit unto holiness, and the end everlasting life.

Colossians 2:13: And you, being dead in your sins and the uncircumcision of your flesh, hath He quickened together with Him.

Hebrews 3:14: For we are made partakers of Christ, if we hold the beginning of our confidence steadfast unto the end.

1 John 3:21: Beloved, if our heart condemn us not, then have we confidence toward God.

WHEN YOU ARE BREAKING FREE
FROM WELFARE/PUBLIC ASSISTANCE

Experience has shown that the more time an able-bodied person spends on public assistance, such as welfare programs, the more likely that person's self-esteem can dissipate into a crippling self-doubt about his or her own abilities to accomplish or succeed.

Further, long-term continuance on such assistance can produce such a dependency on it that the drive to do for one's self is strikingly diminished. In fact, it is not unusual for people on welfare long-term to decrease their more productive activities, such as job searching, down to the mock activity of waiting for their mailpersons to deliver their welfare checks. Due to the potential danger of welfare dependency, chances are great that people on such a system will do better for themselves by working to get free from its false security.

It takes courage and faith to make a triumphant exit from the welfare system to a system designed rather for us to *fare well*. It takes courage to take God at his word when we read 3 John 1:2, which tells us*: Beloved, I wish above all things that thou mayest prosper and be in health, even as thy soul prospereth.* You see, God fully intends for us to fare well by avoiding dependency on systems that could never supply us as He can.

Know that there are people who need you at the place(s) you would be working if you were off welfare and employed. Gather your courage and work to get free!

Power Scriptures for *When You Are Breaking Free From Welfare/Public Assistance*

Deuteronomy 8:18: But thou shalt remember the Lord thy God: for it is He that giveth thee power to get wealth, that He may establish His covenant which He swore unto thy fathers, as it is this day.

2 Chronicles 25:9b: The Lord is able to give thee much more than this.

Isaiah 58:6: Is not this the fast that I have chosen? to loose the bands of wickedness, to undo the heavy burdens, and to let the oppressed go free, and that ye break every yoke?

Psalm 22:19: But be not thou far from me, O Lord: O my strength, haste Thee to help me.

Psalm 37:25: I have been young, and now am old; yet have I not seen the righteous forsaken, nor His seed begging bread.

Psalm 40:17: But I am poor and needy; yet the Lord thinketh upon me: Thou art my help and my deliverer; make no tarrying, O my God.

Psalm 70:5: But I am poor and needy: make haste unto me, O God: Thou art my help and my deliverer; O Lord, make no tarrying.

Psalm 128:2: For thou shalt eat the labor of thine hands: happy shalt thou be, and it shall be well with thee.

Proverbs 10:4: He becometh poor that dealeth with a slack hand: but the hand of the diligent maketh rich.

2 Corinthians 9:8: And God is able to make all grace abound toward you; that ye, always having all sufficiency in all things, may abound to every good work.

Philippians 3:14: I press toward the mark for the prize of the high calling of God in Christ Jesus.

2 Thessalonians 3:8, 10: Neither did we eat any man's bread for nought; but wrought with labor and travail night and day, that we might not be chargeable to any of you: For even when we were with you, this we commanded you, that if any would not work, neither should he eat.

1 Timothy 5:8: But if any provide not for his own, and specially for those of his own house, he hath denied the faith, and is worse than an infidel.

Hebrews 10:38: Now the just shall live by faith: but if any man draw back, My soul shall have no pleasure in him.

Hebrews 11:6: But without faith it is impossible to please Him: for he that cometh to God must believe that He is, and that He is a rewarder of them that diligently seek Him.

WHEN YOU FEEL THAT NO ONE WILL WANT TO HIRE YOU

What is it people see about themselves that convinces them that they have nothing at all to offer employers? If that's something of which you are convinced, have you ever asked yourself why it is that you believe that? Is it possible that you are allowing your mind to replay past experiences where people were harshly critical of your work or of you, and your feelings still negatively impact your self-esteem when you think of those experiences? If so, I recommend that you refuse to continue to rehearse those negative feelings. For when they are rehearsed, they have a nasty habit of derailing any current efforts to become employed. Why is that? Possibly because as the mind goes, so often goes the body.

If a negative past experience is the source of your feeling so poorly about your attractiveness as an employee, please be encouraged to pinpoint the source quickly and to disconnect yourself from its paralyzing effects. The job market is highly competitive, and a confident job candidate is much more attractive to employers than one who mumbles his way through the interview process.

Let us unchain ourselves from whatever tries to convince us that for as long as we live, no employer will *ever* want to hire us (sounds ludicrous, doesn't it?) and get about the business of job searching, free from such a negatively distracting mindset.

Power Scriptures for *When You Feel That No One Will Want to Hire You*

Numbers 13:33: And there we saw the giants, the sons of Anak, which come of the giants: and we were in our own sight as grasshoppers, and so we were in their sight.

Psalm 55:22: Cast thy burden upon the Lord, and He shall sustain thee: He shall never suffer the righteous to be moved.

Psalm 71:21: Thou shalt increase My greatness, and comfort Me on every side.

Proverbs 3:26: For the Lord shall be thy confidence, and shall keep thy foot from being taken.

Isaiah 66:13: As one whom his mother comforteth, so will I comfort you;

Jeremiah 29:11: For I know the thoughts that I think toward you, saith the Lord, thoughts of peace, and not of evil, to give you an expected end.

Jeremiah 32:17: Ah Lord God! behold, Thou hast made the heaven and the earth by Thy great power and stretched out arm, and there is nothing too hard for Thee.

Romans 8:32: He that spared not His own Son, but delivered Him up for us all, how shall He not with Him also freely give us all things?

Romans 12:2: And be not conformed to this world: but be ye transformed by the renewing of your mind, that ye may prove what is that good, and acceptable, and perfect, will of God.

2 Corinthians 3:5: Not that we are sufficient of ourselves to think anything as of ourselves; but our sufficiency is of God.

2 Corinthians 8:12: For if there be first a willing mind, it is accepted according to that a man hath, and not according to that he hath not.

Hebrews 4:3: For we which have believed do enter into rest, as He said, As I have sworn in My wrath, if they shall enter into My rest: although the works were finished from the foundation of the world.

WHEN YOU FEEL YOU ARE TOO OLD TO BE HIRED

When Moses was called by God to lead his people out of the tyrannical control of Pharaoh and into the Promised Land —an energetic mission to be sure —he was 80 years old. And when Moses objected to going because he was concerned about what he saw in himself as an inability to communicate well, God sent an 83-year-old along to speak for him (Aaron). So we know that age is not God's primary consideration when he assigns our purposes or callings, assuming we have taken reasonable care of our "temples" and are, therefore, fairly able-bodied.

So be encouraged not to buy into the over-the-hill mentality that pervades our society's collective thinking. A lot of it is marketing hype for scarcely hidden, financially driven ulterior motives. Rather, prepare yourself to bring interviewers to a place where they buy into the *value* of your age. For instance:

- With a younger interviewer, practice talking about why your age is an *advantage*. For instance, tell how: you've *lived* your lessons —not just read about them in textbooks —and can apply strategies based on experience for damage control long before any potential threat rounds the corner. Rehearse sharing how being from an earlier generation—one known for its loyalty and dedication to commitments—can be an asset to employers.
- To counter stereotypical thinking that older workers are a health risk and/or are not vibrant, rehearse how you can mix in a comment or two about which athletics or exercise method you enjoy in response

to the standard interview opener, *Tell me about yourself.*

- To counter the impression that the 50-and-olders are not innovative, practice responding to: What *kinds of creative or innovative decisions, policies, or strategies did you introduce at your last place of employment? What were the outcomes?*

To help overcome any job-searching bias you may have against your own age group, know that **a)** Your life is not over at age 50 or older; **b)** senior citizens are called that only because they are older than the younger citizens; and **c)** senior and senility *are not* synonymous.

<u>Power Scriptures</u> for *When You Feel You Are Too Old to Be Hired*

Exodus 7:7: And Moses was fourscore [80] years old, and Aaron fourscore and three years old [83], when they spoke unto Pharaoh.

Numbers 13:30b: Let us go up at once, and possess it; for we are well able to overcome it.

Psalm 71:9, 16, 18: Cast me not off in the time of old age; forsake me not when my strength faileth. I will go in the strength of the Lord God: I will make mention of Thy righteousness, even of Thine only. Now also when I am old and grey headed, O God, forsake me not; until I have showed Thy strength unto this generation, and Thy power to every one that is to come.

Psalm 91:16: With long life will I satisfy Him, and show Him my salvation.

Psalm 92:13, 14: Those that be planted in the house of the Lord shall flourish in the courts of our God. They shall still bring forth fruit in old age; they shall be fat and flourishing.

Psalm 10:4, 5: Who redeemeth thy life from destruction; who crowneth thee with loving kindness and tender mercies; Who satisfieth thy mouth with good things; so that thy youth is renewed like the eagle's.

Proverbs 1:31: The hoary head [old age] is a crown of glory, if it be found in the way of righteousness.

Proverbs 19:20: Hear counsel, and receive instruction, that thou mayest be wise in thy latter end.

Proverbs 23:7: For as he thinketh in his heart, so is he.

Isaiah 40:31: But they that wait upon the Lord shall renew their strength; they shall mount up with wings as eagles; they shall run, and not be weary; and they shall walk, and not faint.

Isaiah 4:4: And even to your old age I am He; and even to hoar hairs will I carry you: I have made, and I will bear; even I will carry, and will deliver you.

WHEN YOU FEEL YOU ARE TOO YOUNG TO BE HIRED

David was but a boy when he confronted the giant Goliath. Yet despite David's youth, God empowered him to get the victory. Jesus was a young man in his 30s when He took on the task of being the Savior of the world, yet the Bible says of His accomplishments in John 21:25: ...*there are many other things which Jesus did...the world itself could not contain the books that should be written* (about them).

In the Garden of Gethsemane, Jesus, in order to finish His earthly calling, wrestled with the temptation to be filled with fear and unrest. But He finished His calling anyway for He knew God was with Him. You may be wrestling with fears about being too young to make any significant contribution to a company. However, despite these fears, continue your task (job searching) anyway until you win employment, for God is also *with you.*

To counter feelings that you are too young for an employer to want to hire you, rehearse words similar to those below as if you were responding to the interview question, *"You seem a little young --why should I hire you?"*

- My youth means my mind is pliable and still wide open to strategic brainstorming – after which I have lots of energy to take the ball and run with it!
- I have creativity that is yet unblemished by set, routine thinking that many years of working in any field can produce.
- I grew up using technology. I would, therefore, adapt easily to any need the company may have for workers to learn new software. And I am able to teach others.

As in the cases of David and Jesus—and many others in the Bible—age is not God's primary consideration when placing us into jobs. He simply wants us to be of assistance to others as long as we live. So know that God can use you despite your age, and trust Him to get you placed so you can be used by Him.

Power Scriptures for *When You Feel You Are Young to Be Hired*

Deuteronomy 1:21: Behold, the Lord thy God hath set the land before thee: go up and possess it, as the Lord God of thy fathers hath said unto thee; fear not, neither be discouraged.

Psalm 25:7: Remember not the sins of my youth, nor my transgressions: according to Thy mercy remember Thou me for Thy goodness' sake, O Lord.

Psalm 51:6: Behold, Thou desirest truth in the inward parts: and in the hidden part Thou shalt make me to know wisdom.

Psalm 71:5: For Thou art my hope, O Lord God: Thou art my trust from my youth.

Psalm 71:17: O God, Thou hast taught me from my youth: and hitherto have I declared Thy wondrous works.

Psalm 119:99, 100: I have more understanding than all my teachers: for Thy testimonies are my meditation. I understand more than the ancients, because I keep Thy precepts.

Proverbs 23:12: Apply thine heart unto instruction, and thine ears to the words of knowledge.

Jeremiah 1:6, 7: Then said I, Ah, Lord God! behold, I cannot speak: for I am a child. But the Lord said unto me, Say not, I am a child: for thou shalt go to all that I shall send thee, and whatsoever I command thee thou shalt speak.

1 Timothy 4:12: Let no man despise thy youth; but be thou an example of the believers, in word, in conversation, in charity, in spirit, in faith, in purity.

James 1:5: If any of you lack wisdom, let him ask of God, that giveth to all men liberally, and upbraideth not; and it shall be given him.

1 Peter 5:5: Likewise, ye younger, submit yourselves to the elder. Yea, all of you be subject one to another, and be clothed with humility: for God resisteth the proud, and giveth grace to the humble.

WHEN YOU FEEL YOUR RACE
MAY BE A BARRIER TO BEING HIRED

As we job search, we may be exposed to people who may assign a negative priority to our race or our culture rather than taking a hard look at our skills. Let us understand that we cannot control when or where that will happen without acting to severely limit our job searches. A better strategy is to avoid acts of self-sabotage, whereby we allow another's narrow-mindedness to be our gauge regarding which employers to seek out.

For God's sake, let us check out each opportunity we find to sell our experience and skills to employers. If it is meant for us to work at certain places, it will not matter who approves of our race and who does not. Besides, race disapproval can happen in, say, any supermarket in Apple-Pie, USA. Does that mean we should stop trying to buy food? Oh, we may decide to refrain from buying food from a certain place after a prejudicial experience, but the point is we don't stop food shopping altogether.

Examine yourself. How do you see your own race and/or yourself as a member of it? If you feel inferior, that will be evident the first time you feel a prejudicial attitude directed toward you during an interview. You might, for instance, react to a question about your hair, head wrap, or body wrap or to a "you people" question by becoming defensive instead of with the same patience you would use to respond to any other poorly phrased interview question.

I am not suggesting that we should allow ourselves to be verbally abused during any part of the job search process. What is being suggested is that it may serve us well to come to understand that a person whose thinking is elevated by a healthy self pride in his or her race and/or culture sees prejudiced-based questions and attitudes as ignorant–much like the kinds of questions a child would ask. That type of insight provides a loftier vantage point from which to apply our God-given patience to walk in love toward a possibly prejudiced interviewer. We will then find ourselves more poised to respond calmly and with dignity. We will be more likely to remain focused on winning the position if we fail to respond at gut level to verbal foolishness.

Should you be denied a job and come to suspect that your race clouded the judgment of a potential employer, and you know that you gave your best presentation, then I encourage you to recognize that the interviewer has no idea of what she passed up—a chance to have an ambassador of the living God, complete with his anointing, on her team. Too bad for her! Move on to the next employer by making a graceful, professional exit.

Power Scriptures for *When You Feel Your Race May Be a Barrier to Being Hired*

Joshua 1:9: Have not I commanded thee? Be strong and of a good courage; be not afraid, neither be thou dismayed: for the Lord thy God is with thee whithersoever thou goest.

Psalm 5:12: For thou, Lord, wilt bless the righteous; with favor wilt Thou compass him as with a shield.

Proverbs 13:10: Only by pride cometh contention: but with the well advised is wisdom.

Proverbs 21:1: The king's heart is in the hand of the Lord, as the rivers of water: He turneth it whithersoever He will.

Isaiah 30:15b: ...in quietness and in confidence shall be your strength....

Jeremiah 1:8: Be not afraid of their faces: for I am with thee to deliver thee, saith the Lord.

2 Corinthians 3:17: Now the Lord is that Spirit: and where the Spirit of the Lord is, there is liberty.

2 Thessalonians 3:3: But the Lord is faithful, who shall establish you, and keep you from evil.

Hebrews 13:6: So that we may boldly say, The Lord is my helper, and I will not fear what man shall do unto me.

Titus 2:7, 8: In all things showing thyself a pattern of good works: in doctrine showing uncorruptness, gravity, sincerity. Sound speech, that cannot be condemned; that he that is of the contrary part may be ashamed, having no evil thing to say of you.

1 Peter 2:9, 15: But ye are a chosen generation, a royal priesthood, an holy nation, a peculiar people; that ye should show forth the praises of Him who hath called you out of darkness into His marvelous light; for so is the will of God, that with well doing ye may put to silence the ignorance of foolish men.

1 Peter 3:13: And who is he that will harm you, if ye be followers of that which is good?

WHEN YOU NEED CONFIDENCE
TO JOB SEARCH AFTER A MEDICAL DISABILITY

Have you recently been released by a doctor to return to the workplace? Have you prayerfully considered whether you *should* return? Do you have a handle on which skills are your strong suits and which need further development? If you answered *yes* to each question, then more than likely you are ready to reenter the job market after your medical disability.

After the interviewing process begins, and after you have disclosed that you are returning to the job market after recovering from a long-term illness, you may sense that an employer is thinking that you would be a risky hire. Here's a strategy for deflecting attention from a past sickness and on to your skills where it belongs. Without so much as a hint of trepidation in your tone, offer that you have been totally cleared (or briefly state the restrictions) by your doctor to go back to work, and then name the skills you are ready to contribute to the company. Be prepared to provide your doctor's release.

Should you bear any apparent mark on your body from a previous illness or disability and an employer's eyes settle on it, bravely and goodnaturedly offer with a smile that you are otherwise attractive— as in your creative ability; in your ability to send sales and profit through the roof; or in your ability to overcome challenges and still succeed. In other words, help potential employers see you as having equal footing (at least mentally if not physically) with other job seekers, despite any past infirmity.

I pray that your confidence for job searching is buoyed and that you grow ever stronger as you embark upon your journey to find employment.

Power Scriptures for *When You Need Confidence to Job Search After a Medical Disability*

Job 4:3, 4: Behold, thou hast instructed many, and thou hast strengthened the weak hands. Thy words have upheld him that was falling, and Thou hast strengthened the feeble knees.

Psalm 22:19: But be not Thou far from me, O Lord: O my strength, haste Thee to help me.

Psalm 30:2: O Lord my God, I cried unto Thee, and Thou hast healed me.

Psalm 107:20: He sent His word, and healed them, and delivered them from their destructions.

Psalm 116:8-10: For Thou hast delivered my soul from death, mine eyes from tears, and my feet from falling. I will walk before the Lord in the land of the living. I believed, therefore have I spoken....

Psalm 138:3: In the day when I cried Thou answeredst me, and strengthenedst me with strength in my soul.

Isaiah 41:10: Fear thou not; for I am with thee: be not dismayed; for I am thy God: I will strengthen thee; yea, I will help thee; yea, I will uphold thee with the right hand of my righteousness.

Isaiah 53:5: But He was wounded for our transgressions, He was bruised for our iniquities: the chastisement of our peace was upon Him; and with His stripes we are healed.

Jeremiah 17:14: Heal me, O Lord, and I shall be healed; save me, and I shall be saved: for Thou art my praise.

Matthew 8:13: And Jesus said unto the centurion, Go thy way; and as thou hast believed, so be it done unto thee. And His servant was healed in the selfsame hour.

Mark 1:34: And He healed many that were sick of divers diseases....

Philippians 4:13: I can do all things through Christ which strengtheneth me.

WHEN CHOOSING PEOPLE FOR NETWORKING

We all know that a network of people is defined (in part) as an *interrelated group* of people. An ideal model of an effective interrelated group for unemployed people is comprised of those who: 1) can feed them information about job openings that they may not otherwise be privy to, 2) are able to help them practice their interviewing techniques, help with resume writing, etc., and 3) are willing to pay, say, a late bill for them and forgive the debt until they get back on their feet. But there is one more quality we should look for when seeking to surround ourselves with a network for support when facing unemployment: those who can encourage us in our faith. In other words, our ideal network of people would minister to both our physical and spiritual needs.

To gather such support, we must not withdraw from people but instead allow ourselves to be open and honest with others about our needs. Don't allow your pride to talk you out of obeying this book's fourth commandment for a successful job search: *Assemble Yourself with Believers* (see Section 2, Part 2). Besides, when we don't express our needs to others, we are behaving selfishly. How can that be?

When we allow others a chance to minister to our needs in our difficult times, we become conduits for them to receive the blessings of God in their own lives in return for their having blessed us. So let us ask God to surround us with supporters who can minister to both our physical and spiritual needs. And let's resolve to return the favor we receive in our hours of need to others when it is our turn to help.

Consider Proverbs 27:17: *Iron sharpeneth iron; so a man sharpeneth the countenance of his friend.*

Power Scriptures for *When Choosing People for Networking*

Psalm 1:1: Blessed is the man that walketh not in the counsel of the ungodly, nor standeth in the way of sinners, nor sitteth in the seat of the scornful.

Psalm 118:8: It is better to trust in the Lord than to put confidence in man.

Proverbs 1:5: A wise man will hear, and will increase learning; and a man of understanding shall attain unto wise counsels.

Proverbs 14:7: Go from the presence of a foolish man, when thou perceivest not in him the lips of knowledge.

Proverbs 19:20: Hear counsel, and receive instruction, that thou mayest be wise in thy latter end.

Proverbs 20:18: Every purpose is established by counsel.

Proverbs 25:19: Confidence in an unfaithful man in time of trouble is like a broken tooth, and a foot out of joint.

Matthew 7:16: Ye shall know them by their fruits. Do men gather grapes of thorns, or figs of thistles?

Matthew 12:35: A good man out of the good treasure of the heart bringeth forth good things: and an evil man out of the evil treasure bringeth forth evil things.

Luke 21:19: In your patience possess ye your souls.

2 Corinthians 10:5: Casting down imaginations, and every high thing that exalteth itself against the knowledge of God, and bringing into captivity every thought to the obedience of Christ.

Colossians 2:8: Beware lest any man spoil you through philosophy and vain deceit, after the tradition of men, after the rudiments of the world, and not after Christ.

James 3:17: But the wisdom that is from above is first pure, then peaceable, gentle, and easy to be entreated, full of mercy and good fruits, without partiality, and without hypocrisy.

WHEN YOU HAVE BEEN A LONG TIME JOB SEARCHING

Do you remember how long Abraham waited for his dream of being the father of many nations to come to pass? Twenty years. Jesus was 12 when he announced to his parents that he had to be about his Father's business— then it was approximately 18 years later before he actually walked out his calling. Why didn't God's obvious will for both of these men come to pass earlier, when each already understood what God's will was? More than likely it was because there is a huge difference between how God sees time and how we see it.

Time for us is sort of a period of marked existence. That is, we can check a mechanism, usually a watch or clock, to see which of our 1,440 minutes each day or of our 24 hours we have entered or are exiting. We tend to move—start activities, rush them, slow them, get frustrated while doing them, or end them—based on what we see on a watch or a clock.

However, there is strong evidence in the Bible that God tends to see time as a *process* and that He acts more on *timing* than on time itself. That is, it seems that he assigns time to contain activities for us. And when we get to where He needs us to be, spiritually and naturally speaking, we are released into the activity at a pre-set point in time. Consider Ecclesiastes 3:1: To *everything there is a season, and a time to every purpose under the heaven.* (Also see Section 2, Part 1 on *Seven Possible Reasons for Prolonged Unemployment.)*

While we may not be able to tell the precise moment when we will finally win employment, one thing is sure: If we give up, we never will win. Those who truly believe God for work never give up.

Power Scriptures for *When You Have Been a Long Time Job Searching*

Psalm 5:1-3: Give ear to my words, O Lord, consider my meditation. Hearken unto the voice of my cry, my King, and my God: for unto Thee will I pray. My voice shalt Thou hear in the morning, O Lord; in the morning will I direct my prayer unto Thee, and will look up.

Psalm 27:13, 14: I had fainted, unless I had believed to see the goodness of the Lord in the land of the living. Wait on the Lord: be of good courage, and He shall strengthen thine heart: wait, I say, on the Lord.

Psalm 29:11: The Lord will give strength unto His people; the Lord will bless His people with peace.

Psalm 34:18: The Lord is nigh unto them that are of a broken heart; and saveth such as be of a contrite spirit.

Psalm 73:26: My flesh and my heart faileth: but God is the strength of my heart, and my portion forever.

Psalm 102:1, 2, 4, 17: Hear my prayer, O Lord, and let my cry come unto Thee. Hide not Thy face from me in the day when I am in trouble; incline Thine ear unto me: in the day when I call answer me speedily...He will regard the prayer of the destitute, and not despise their prayer.

Psalm 138:3: In the day when I cried Thou answeredst me, and strengthenedst me with strength in my soul.

Ecclesiastes 3:1: To every thing there is a season, and a time to every purpose under the heaven.

Isaiah 40:31: But they that wait upon the Lord shall renew their strength; they shall mount up with wings as eagles; they shall run, and not be weary; and they shall walk, and not faint.

Jeremiah 29:11: For I know the thoughts that I think toward you, saith the Lord, thoughts of peace, and not of evil, to give you an expected end.

Jeremiah 31:13b: ...I will turn their mourning into joy, and will comfort them, and make them rejoice from their sorrow.

Luke 21:19: In Your patience possess Ye Your souls.

1 Corinthians 9:24: Know ye not that they which run in a race run all, but one receiveth the prize? So run, that ye may obtain.

2 Corinthians 2:14: Now thanks be unto God, which always causeth us to triumph in Christ, and maketh manifest the savour of His knowledge by us in every place.

Hebrews 10:23: Let us hold fast the profession of our faith without wavering; [for he is faithful that promised].

WHEN YOU FEEL YOU CANNOT TITHE

Let's say you gave a person you loved $100. Then you asked if he would give $10 of it to benefit someone else. What would you think about that person if he refused to give up $10 even after you told him: a) it was needed to benefit someone else in dire need, and b) that you would repay him *a lot more* than the $10? Would you consider him to be a stingy or selfish person—or perhaps an ingrate—if he continued to refuse to share? That's probably how we seem to God when we decide we will not tithe.

It may help us to be more willing to share if we keep in mind that a Person who "lives" in a place where there are streets of gold and gates made of pearl does not need our money personally. What God is asking is that we share what He's given us in order to get the true riches -- knowledge of Himself, his Son, and of Holy Spirit —made known to others. He considers those who don't know Him to be in dire need. He uses our money through others for practical stuff, like keeping the lights on in places where people can come to find Him, to learn, and to worship.

You don't have an income, you say, so how can you tithe? Remember that God judges the purposes and the intents of the heart. If you have a heart to tithe, and you have a quarter, give three cents of it (tithe means one-tenth). Pray over those three pennies before dropping them in the offering bucket as if you were putting in a million dollars. Can't spare the three cents? Can you give two? Start where you can, and if your heart is right, He will increase what you have more and more. Remember how Jesus was moved by the widow who gave the two mites from the little she had while others with more were giving a whole lot more? It was her heart that pleased Him more than the large amounts others were giving.

Tithing is a sign to God that you trust Him so much to take care of you that you are willing to share what you have. By sharing you demonstrate to God that He and His cause to win others to Himself are more important to you than how much money you currently do or do not have.

Power Scriptures for *When You Feel You Cannot Tithe*

Proverbs 8:17-21: I love them that love Me; and those that seek Me early shall find Me. Riches and honor are with Me; yea, durable riches and righteousness. My fruit is better than gold, yea, than fine gold; and My revenue than choice silver. I lead in the way of righteousness, in the midst of the paths of judgment: That I may cause those that love Me to inherit substance; and I will fill their treasures.

Proverbs 11:25: The liberal [generous] soul shall be made fat [prosperous] and he that watereth shall be watered also himself.

75

Psalm 16:5: The Lord is the portion of mine inheritance and of my cup: Thou maintainest my lot.

Psalm 118:25: Save now, I beseech Thee, O Lord: O Lord, I beseech Thee, send now prosperity.

Proverbs 19:17: He that hath pity upon the poor lendeth unto the Lord; and that which he hath given will He pay him again.

Proverbs 21:13: Whoso stoppeth his ears at the cry of the poor, he also shall cry himself, but shall not be heard.

Luke 6:38: Give, and it shall be given unto you; good measure, pressed down, and shaken together, and running over, shall men give into your bosom. For with the same measure that ye mete withal it shall be measured to you again.

Luke 21:1-3: And He [Jesus] looked up, and saw the rich men casting their gifts into the treasury. And He saw also a certain poor widow casting in thither two mites. And He said, Of a truth I say unto you, that this poor widow hath cast in more than they all.

2 Corinthians 8:12: For if there be first a willing mind, it is accepted according to that a man hath, and not according to that he hath not.

2 Corinthians 9:7: Every man according as he purposeth in his heart, so let him give; not grudgingly, or of necessity: for God loveth a cheerful giver.

WHEN TEMPTED TO GAIN INCOME ILLEGALLY

The temptation to do other than honest labor as a means for gaining income for our needs is usually born of a fear that we will not be able to get the money we need otherwise. Remember when God promised Abraham that he would be the father of many nations? And how, after waiting many years and no child was yet on the way, Abraham followed his wife's plan to "help" God make the promise come true by "knowing" his wife's handmaiden? (See Genesis 16.) A child was born (Ishmael) but not the child of promise (Isaac).

Participating in activities that don't befit an ambassador of Christ for whatever reason has the potential to create Ishmaels, that is, end results that are not the will of God. And while God did care for Ishmael and did go on to bless Abraham to beget Isaac and allowed him to be the father of many nations as he had promised, Ishmael's birth was not God's perfect will for Abraham.

Likewise, God will not desert us should we get locked up for breaking the law. But I'll venture that He would rather we trust Him enough to provide for our needs so that we don't get pulled off course by having to serve time behind bars. Some may argue that otherwise good people who get locked up for, say, stealing acted in accordance with God's design. Their argument might be that they got locked up because of a divine plan to position themselves to minister to the incarcerated. I submit that while it may be true that He wants us to minister to prisoners, it is also true that since God is in the setting-captives-free business, he wants us to be able to *leave* the prison *at will* once we are done ministering!

Let's be unwilling to trade His good name, which we bear, for any ill-gotten gain through questionable activities. Consider Proverbs 20:21: *An inheritance* [possessions, property, things] *may be gotten hastily* [including through anxiousness or from greed] *at the beginning; but the end thereof shall not be blessed.*

<u>Power Scriptures</u> for *When Tempted to Gain Income Illegally*

Proverbs 11:27: He that diligently seeketh good procureth favor: but he that seeketh mischief, it shall come unto him.

Proverbs 16:25: There is a way that seemeth right unto a man, but the end thereof are the ways of death.

Proverbs 29:24: Whoso is partner with a thief hateth his own soul.

Romans 6:2, 11, 13, 20: God forbid. How shall we, that are dead to sin, live any longer therein? Likewise reckon ye also yourselves to be dead indeed unto sin, but alive unto God through Jesus Christ our Lord. Neither yield ye your members as instruments of unrighteousness unto sin: but yield yourselves unto God.... For when ye were the servants of sin, ye were free from righteousness.

Ephesians 5:15, 17: See then that ye walk circumspectly, not as fools, but as wise....Wherefore be ye not unwise, but understanding what the will of the Lord is.

1 Corinthians 10:13: There hath no temptation taken you but such as is common to man: but God is faithful, who will not suffer you to be tempted above that ye are able; but will with the temptation also make a way to escape, that ye may be able to bear it.

Colossians 3:25: But he that doeth wrong shall receive for the wrong which he hath done: and there is no respect of persons.

Hebrews 2:8a: Thou hast put all things in subjection under His feet. For in that He put all in subjection under Him, He left nothing that is not put under Him.

1 John 3:22: And whatsoever we ask, we receive of Him, because we keep His commandments, and do those things that are pleasing in His sight.

WHEN TEMPTED TO LIE ABOUT YOUR ABILITIES

Why do otherwise truthful people sometimes lie about their abilities when they are job searching? One reason stems from a fear that some truth about their work histories may cost them an opportunity to be hired. Also, people sometimes look at their skills and decide that they have to augment them with falsehoods in order to make themselves more appealing to employers. But lying words cannot profit us (see Jeremiah 7:8). In fact, lies have a nasty habit of boomeranging back on us at the most inopportune time. But if we throw lying words out, they can't circle back around to hurt us or others.

For instance, suppose you lied about being able to accomplish tasks using a certain software program, which was listed as a required skill when you applied for the job, and the employer believed you had the skill and hired you. And let's say that somewhere down the road, it is discovered that not only do you not have a clue about the program but that you have been burdening others with questions about its simplest functions. The employer may end up being disappointed in you (and in himself for being duped by you during the interview). And you may find yourself fired for falsifying your information.

That means that *one* lie caused: 1) a chink in someone else's esteem; 2) wasted dollars that were paid for staff and materials to process your application, your medical test, etc.; and 3) a dark shadow over your character —your integrity.

Let us be guided by Proverbs 19:5, which says that *a false witness shall not be unpunished, and he that speaks lies shall not escape.* Believers and faith-seekers alike would do well to be mindful of the words of 2 Corinthians 5:20: *Now then we are ambassadors for Christ.* Lying contradicts an ideal representation of Christ to the world.

Power Scriptures for *When Tempted to Lie About Your Abilities*

Job 27:4: My lips shall not speak wickedness, nor my tongue utter deceit.

Job 3:3: My words shall be of the uprightness of my heart: and my lips shall utter knowledge clearly.

Job 6:24: Teach me, and I will hold my tongue: and cause me to understand wherein I have erred.

Psalm 120:2: Deliver my soul, O Lord, from lying lips, and from a
deceitful tongue.

Psalm 141:3: Set a watch, O Lord, before my mouth; keep the door of my lips.

Proverbs 18:21: Death and life are in the power of the tongue: and they that love it shall eat the fruit thereof.

Proverbs 12:19, 22: The lip of truth shall be established forever: but a lying tongue is but for a moment. Lying lips are abomination to the Lord: but they that deal truly are his delight.

Proverbs 16:13: Righteous lips are the delight of kings; and they love Him that speaketh right.

Proverbs 21:6: The getting of treasures by a lying tongue is a vanity tossed to and fro of them that seek death.

Jeremiah 7:8: Behold, ye trust in lying words, that cannot profit.

Ephesians 4:29: Let no corrupt communication proceed out of your mouth, but that which is good to the use of edifying, that it may minister grace unto the hearers.

Colossians 3:9, 10: Lie not one to another, seeing that ye have put off the old man with his deeds; and have put on the new man, which is renewed in knowledge after the image of Him that created him.

WHEN AFRAID TO INTERVIEW

People who are afraid to interview for jobs usually believe one or more of the following:

- That they would not know how to respond to questions (despite having the ability to respond to all kinds of questions perfectly well until they are categorized as "interview questions");
- That their nerves would get in the way, and they would end up speaking gibberish and looking foolish (despite having had occasion to speak gibberish before and look foolish, yet still manage to make things turn out just fine—as in the case of a first date, for instance);
- That they wouldn't have the right skills or experience for the job (despite the fact that most people don't

81

apply for jobs for which they have *zero* skills—so it's just a matter of being well-rehearsed in the skills they do have).

What these fears have in common is that once a person is convinced that they are legitimate, they *become* true for them; and they begin to behave in accordance with these so-called truths. A fear-filled job applicant manifests fear during the most inopportune time, usually in front of employers, despite how hard they attempt to mask it. Not a pretty sight for employers to witness. So in the words of Deuteronomy 31:6: *Be strong and of a good courage...nor be afraid of them: for the Lord thy God, He it is that doth go with thee; He will not fail thee, nor forsake thee.*

Power Scriptures for *When Afraid to Interview*

Exodus 4:10-12: And Moses said unto the Lord, O my Lord, I am not eloquent, neither heretofore, nor since Thou hast spoken unto Thy servant: but I am slow of speech, and of a slow tongue. And the Lord said unto him, Who hath made man's mouth? or who maketh the dumb, or deaf, or the seeing, or the blind? have not I the Lord? Now therefore go, and I will be with thy mouth, and teach thee what thou shalt say.

Job 33:3: My words shall be of the uprightness of my heart: and my lips shall utter knowledge clearly.

Proverbs 12:14: A man shall be satisfied with good by the fruit of his mouth: and the recompense of a man's hands shall be rendered unto him.

Proverbs 16:23: The heart of the wise teacheth his mouth, and addeth learning to his lips.

Psalm 49:3: My mouth shall speak of wisdom; and the meditation of my heart shall be of understanding.

Psalm 56:3: What time I am afraid, I will trust in Thee.

Psalm 94:19: In the multitude of my thoughts within me Thy comforts delight my soul.

Psalm 141:3: Set a watch, O Lord, before my mouth; keep the door of my lips.

Proverbs 16:18, 24: Pride goeth before destruction, and an haughty spirit before a fall. Pleasant words are as a honeycomb, sweet to the soul, and health to the bones.

Proverbs 29:11, 29: A fool uttereth all his mind: but a wise man keepeth it in till afterwards. Seest thou a man that is hasty in his words? there is more hope of a fool than of him.

Isaiah 26:3: Thou wilt keep him in perfect peace, whose mind is stayed on Thee: because he trusteth in Thee.

Isaiah 32:4b: ...the tongue of the stammerers shall be ready to speak plainly.

Isaiah 51:7: Hearken unto Me, ye that know righteousness, the people in whose heart is My law; fear ye not the reproach of men, neither be ye afraid of their revilings.

Luke 1:12: For the Holy Ghost shall teach you in the same hour what ye ought to say.

1 Corinthians 2:4: And My speech and My preaching was not with enticing words of man's wisdom, but in demonstration of the Spirit and of power.

Colossians 4:6: Let your speech be always with grace, seasoned with salt, that ye may know how ye ought to answer every man.

James 1:19: Wherefore, my beloved brethren, let every man be swift to hear, slow to speak.

WHEN FACED WITH UNPROVOKED HOSTILITY FROM PROSPECTIVE CO-WORKERS

Inherent in the nature of humans is a need to protect what is perceived to be theirs. It starts in childhood. If a child approaches a second child out of curiosity to play with the first's toys, it isn't an uncommon sight to see the owner of the toys enclose them in his arms or otherwise hold onto them tightly. He may even punctuate his action with a stubborn declaration of "Mine!" Similarly, there may be instances where you'll walk into a prospective place of employment to complete an application and/or to interview and find yourself, despite your obvious friendliness, met with hostility from those who would be your co-workers.

Unprovoked hostility often stems from the hostile ones' fear of loss, which, in turn, may raise a need in them to guard their "territories" aggressively. It is their way of proclaiming "Mine!" about their jobs. There are reasons for unprovoked hostility. For instance, a hostile person may have applied for the same position for which you are applying, and your presence announces that someone else could win that job. Or it could be something as simple as the fact that the hostile one considers you more attractive them him/herself, and so your presence knocks at his/her self-esteem.

Or perhaps the offender is simply having a bad day— or a bad life. To have to figure out the reasons for every occasion of unprovoked hostility of others is to be distracted from the task at hand, which is to get employed. Ask God to teach you how to respond with wisdom to hostile people. And remain professionally friendly for the sake of shining your peace onto others, demanding nothing from others in return. Stay focused on winning the position.

Power Scriptures for *When Faced with Unprovoked Hostility from Prospective Co-Workers*

Psalm 33:10: The Lord bringeth the counsel of the heathen to nought: He maketh the devices of the people of none effect.

Psalm 56:11: In God have I put my trust: I will not be afraid [of] what man can do unto me.

Psalm 71:4, 13: Deliver me, O my God, out of the hand of the wicked, out of the hand of the unrighteous and cruel man. Let them be confounded and consumed that are adversaries to my soul; let them be covered with reproach and dishonor that seek my hurt.

Psalm 119:110: The wicked have laid a snare for me: yet I erred not from Thy precepts.

Psalm 119:86: All Thy commandments are faithful: they persecute me wrongfully; help Thou me.

Proverbs 16:7, 32: When a man's ways please the Lord, He maketh even his enemies to be at peace with him. He that is slow to anger is better than the mighty; and he that ruleth his spirit than he that taketh a city.

Proverbs 19:11: The discretion of a man deferreth his anger; and it is his glory to pass over a transgression.

Jeremiah 1:8: Be not afraid of their faces: for I am with thee to deliver thee, saith the Lord.

Luke 6:27, 31: But I say unto you which hear, love your enemies, do good to them which hate you...and as ye would that men should do to you, do ye also to them likewise.

2 Thessalonians 1:4, 6: So that we ourselves glory in You in the churches of God for Your patience and faith in all your persecutions and tribulations that Ye endure: Seeing it is a righteous thing with God to recompense tribulation to them that trouble You.

Titus 2:7, 8: In all things showing thyself a pattern of good works: in doctrine showing uncorruptness, gravity, sincerity, Sound speech, that cannot be condemned; that he that is of the contrary part may be ashamed, having no evil thing to say of you.

1 Peter 2:9, 15: But ye are a chosen generation, a royal priesthood, an holy nation, a peculiar people; that ye should show forth the praises of Him who hath called you out of darkness into His marvelous light. For so is the will of God, that with well doing ye may put to silence the ignorance of foolish men.

WHEN FACING REJECTION FROM EMPLOYERS

Wouldn't it be wonderful if everyone who has to judge us regarding our personalities, behaviors, and skills —such as prospective employers —made only positive comments about us, even when we fell short? Since that is not going to happen, it is up to us to decide long before beginning the interviewing process exactly to what extent we will allow the comments of others to impact our drive to succeed.

It may help to understand that being rejected for a job, for a part in a play, or by a boyfriend or girlfriend can happen to anyone and is a normal part of the human experience of choice making. The facts are, we all have experienced rejection, and rejection in and of itself is not a bad thing. But it becomes a bad thing *in us* if we internalize the reasons for the rejection and begin to replace our healthy opinions about ourselves with unhealthy, destructive ones.

Purposely decide that you will prayerfully consider incorporating what you learn from constructive criticism and will disregard the rest. By analyzing presentations you made to employers who turned you down, you may find ways to improve your performance. Your esteem will remain in tact, and you will be better able to move forward with the wisdom of lessons learned in tow.

Power Scriptures for *When Facing Rejection from Employers*

Psalm 3:3: But thou, O Lord, art a shield for me; my Glory, and the lifter up of mine head.

Psalm 42:11: Why art thou cast down, O my soul? and why art thou disquieted within me? Hope thou in God...who is the health of my countenance, and my God.

Psalm 55:22: Cast thy burden upon the Lord, and He shall sustain thee: He shall never suffer the righteous to be moved.

Psalm 126:5: They that sow in tears shall reap in joy.

Psalm 143:11: Quicken me, O Lord, for Thy name's sake: for Thy righteousness' sake bring my soul out of trouble.

Proverbs 3:26: For the Lord shall be thy confidence.

Proverbs 25:28: He that hath no rule over his own **spirit is like a city that is broken down, and without walls.**

Proverbs 29:25: The fear of man bringeth a snare: but whoso putteth his trust in the Lord shall be safe.

Matthew 10:14: And whosoever shall not receive you, nor hear your words, when ye depart out of that house or city, shake off the dust of your feet.

Luke 20:17: And He beheld them, and said, What is this then that is written, The stone which the builders rejected, the same is become the head of the corner?

Romans 8:37: …In all these things we are more than conquerors through Him that loved us.

2 Corinthians 1:7: And our hope of you is steadfast, knowing, that as ye are partakers of the sufferings, so shall ye be also of the consolation.

Philippians 1:6: Being confident of this very thing, that he which hath begun a good work in you will perform it until the day of Jesus Christ.

Hebrews 13:6: So that we may boldly say, The Lord is my helper, and I will not fear what man shall do unto me.

1 John 5:4: For whatsoever is born of God overcometh the world: and this is the victory that overcometh the world, even our faith.

WHEN TEMPTED TO RELIEVE FRUSTRATIONS BY ABUSING SUBSTANCES

We could eat until we are ready to burst; we could drink alcohol until we can't stand up; we could take illegal *or* legal drugs until we can't think straight —but when the effects of these substances wear off, we would still have the same frustrations we had before we abused those substances. And our bodies, God's temples, would be left with the havoc these "relievers" wreak.

Rather than trying to escape our troubles via the assorted poisons readily available in the world, let us relieve the frustrations of our challenges by taking "gos-pills." "Gos-pills," scriptures from the Bible, as well as those powerful, positive sayings from our society's greatest leaders, can be very effective frustration relievers —our pain pills —when "taken" with regularity and in faith.

For instance, we could take a daily dose of Psalm 138:3: *In the day when I cried Thou answeredst me, and strengthenedst me with strength in my soul, every hour on the hour.* Every night, we could drink in an eyeful of Psalm 46:1: *God is our refuge and strength, a very present help in trouble.* And while giving thanks is sometimes the last thing we tend to want to do when we're frustrated, let us minister doses of thanksgiving to God freely throughout the day. We are not thanking Him for our difficulties. Rather, we are thanking Him for seeing us through past troubles as well as for His promised faithfulness for escorting us through the present trouble.

If we take our "gos-pills" faithfully, prayerfully, we will be less likely to abuse those other so-called pain "relievers." Our minds will then remain sharp for the task at hand: finding employment.

Power Scriptures for *When Tempted to Relieve Frustrations by Abusing Substances*

Psalm 107:20: He sent His word, and healed them, and delivered them from their destructions.

Isaiah 40:29: He giveth power to the faint; and to them that have no might He increaseth strength.

Ephesians 6:11: Put on the whole armor of God, that ye may be able to stand against the wiles of the devil.

89

Romans 6:12: Let not sin therefore reign in your mortal body, that ye should obey it in the lusts thereof.

1 Corinthians 6:19, 20: What? know ye not that your body is the temple of the Holy Ghost which is in you, which ye have of God, and ye are not your own? For ye are bought with a price: therefore glorify God in your body, and in your spirit, which are God's.

1 Corinthians 10:23: All things are lawful for Me, but all things are not expedient: all things are lawful for Me, but all things edify not.

2 Timothy 2:21: If a man therefore purge himself from these, he shall be a vessel unto honor, sanctified, and meet for the Master's use, and prepared unto every good work.

James 1:12-14: Blessed is the man that endureth temptation: for when he is tried, he shall receive the crown of life, which the Lord hath promised to them that love Him. Let no man say when he is tempted, I am tempted of God: for God cannot be tempted with evil, neither tempteth He any man: But every man is tempted, when he is drawn away of his own lust, and enticed.

1 Peter 5:8: Be sober, be vigilant; because your adversary the devil, as a roaring lion, walketh about, seeking whom he may devour.

2 Peter 2:9: The Lord knoweth how to deliver the godly out of temptations.

Haggai 1:6, 7: Ye have sown much, and bring in little; ye eat, but ye have not enough; ye drink, but ye are not filled with drink; ye clothe you, but there is none warm; and he that earneth wages earneth wages to put it into a bag with holes. Thus saith the Lord of hosts; Consider your ways.

WHEN YOU NEED ASSURANCE OF EVENTUAL SUCCESS

Since God is not likely to open our ceilings and rain employers down on us when we desire work, the search for work will have to become our new job until we can find another one. In fact, Ecclesiastes 5:3 tells us that: ...*a dream comes true through the <u>multitude</u> of business.* For our purposes here, that means we as job seekers will have to be about the task of job searching diligently to be best assured of eventual success.

Some "what's-the-use" types might ask (especially those experiencing protracted job searches), How can we be sure that after doing all that it takes to find a job—studying our skills, going back into the classroom as necessary, gathering and fortifying our employment documents—God will provide us with new employment? In response I would ask two other questions: How can we be sure that He *won't*; and how will we find out if we stop trying?

One other thought: know that it is very difficult for most people to stand strong and long in faith over any issue when they think they don't deserve to be answered. If you are doing all it takes to find a job but you are impenitent in some area that you know God needs you to clear up with Him, by not doing so you could impede the answers to your prayers. So why not go ahead and get that clog of offense out of the way so you can believe God for work with a faith strong enough to last until employment is won. (See Section 2, Part 1: *Seven Possible Reasons for Prolonged Unemployment.*)

Be assured that your turn to win an employment offer will come. But you can't give up because quitters *can't* win.

Allow the words of Ecclesiastes 3:1 to anchor your patience: *To every thing there is a season, and a time to every purpose under the heaven.*

Power Scriptures for *When You Need Assurance of Eventual Success*

Deuteronomy 11:13, 14: And it shall come to pass, if ye shall hearken diligently unto My commandments which I command you this day, to love the Lord your God, and to serve Him with all your heart and with all your soul, That I will give you the rain of your land in his due season, the first rain and the later rain, that thou mayest gather in thy corn, and thy wine, and thine oil.

Joshua 1:8: This book of the law shall not depart out of thy mouth; but thou shalt meditate therein day and night, that thou mayest observe to do according to all that is written therein: for then thou shalt make thy way prosperous, and then thou shalt have good success.

Psalm 1:2, 3: But his delight is in the law of the Lord; and in His law doth he meditate day and night. And he shall be like a tree planted by the rivers of water, that bringeth forth his fruit in his season; his leaf also shall not wither; and whatsoever he doeth shall prosper.

Ecclesiastes 11:6: In the morning sow thy seed, and in the evening withhold not thine hand: for thou knowest not whether shall prosper, either this or that, or whether they both shall be alike good.

Isaiah 58:11: And the Lord shall guide thee continually, and satisfy thy soul in drought, and make fat thy bones: and thou shalt be like a watered garden, and like a spring of water, whose waters fail not.

Galatians 6:9: And let us not be weary in well doing: for in due season we shall reap, if we faint not.

Hebrews 6:11, 12: And we desire that every one of you do show the same diligence to the full assurance of hope unto the end: That ye be not slothful, but followers of them who through faith and patience inherit the promises.

2 Peter 1:10: Wherefore the rather, brethren, give diligence to make your calling and election sure: for if ye do these things, ye shall never fall.

WHEN YOU RECEIVE AN UNDESERVED LOW RATING ON A REFERENCE FORM OR LETTER

When we are treated unjustly, we can take one of two actions: 1) strike back – possibly injuring someone either physically or emotionally—thereby draining our own energy and the focus we need for the job search; or 2) understand that no weapon formed against us shall prosper, pray to God to protect us from liars and the effects of their words, and decide to take no retaliatory action against the person.

Since as believers we are encouraged to practice behaving toward others with love, we have to determine even before we are confronted with an unjust criticism that we will respond in ways that honor the Name by which we are called.

So what might you do should you find yourself faced with a character attack during an interview? Consider the following:

The lie stated: Your former employer says here that you were unproductive....

Your response: That is not an accurate assessment. For instance, I was especially productive in the area of... *name it and provide back-up information such as statistics, etc.)*

How can a person learn to be so forbearing when experiencing the frustrations of unjust slander? Cooperate with the sweet Spirit within us to develop an ability to be patient and in control of our temper. Tap into the fruit of the Spirit in accordance with Galatians 5:22, 23, 25, which says in part: ...*the fruit of the Spirit is love, joy, peace, long suffering, gentleness, goodness, faith...meekness, temperance: against such there is no law. If we live in the Spirit, let us also walk in the Spirit.* Rest assured that vengeance is not only the Lord's but that He will repay, as Romans 12:19 states.

This frees us from having to spend energy on devising retaliatory schemes. We can remain focused on job searching. If we are truly innocent of all charges, we can offer faith-filled prayers that there will be no everlasting effect of their lies upon our opportunities.

Avoid the temptation to pay ill will back with ill will.

Power Scriptures for *When You Receive an Undeserved Low Rating on a Reference Form or Letter*

Psalm 25:2: My God, I trust in Thee: let me not be ashamed, let not mine enemies triumph over me.

Psalm 33:10: The Lord bringeth the counsel of the heathen to nought: He maketh the devices of the people of none effect.

Psalm 56:11: So shall I have wherewith to answer him that reproacheth me: for I trust in Thy word.

Psalm 70:2, 3: Let them be ashamed and confounded that seek after my soul: let them be turned backward, and put to confusion, that desire my hurt. Let them be turned back for a reward of their shame that say, Aha, aha.

Psalm 71:4, 13, 24: Deliver me, O my God, out of the hand of the wicked, out of the hand of the unrighteous and cruel man. Let them be confounded and consumed that are adversaries to my soul; let them be covered with reproach and dishonor that seek my hurt. My tongue also shall talk of Thy righteousness all the day long: for they are confounded, for they are brought unto shame, that seek my hurt.

Psalm 83:1, 16: Keep not Thou silence, O God: hold not Thy peace, and be not still, O God. Fill their faces with shame; that they may seek Thy name, O Lord.

Psalm 140:4: Keep me, O Lord, from the hands of the wicked; preserve me from the violent man; who have purposed to overthrow my goings.

Psalm 141:10: Let the wicked fall into their own nets, whilst that I withal escape.

Proverbs 19:5, 9: A false witness shall not be unpunished, and he that speaketh lies shall not escape. A false witness shall not be unpunished, and he that speaketh lies shall perish.

Proverbs 26:27: Whoso diggeth a pit shall fall therein: and he that rolleth a stone, it will return upon him.

Proverbs 30:5: Every word of God is pure: He is a shield unto them that put their trust in Him.

Isaiah 54:17: No weapon that is formed against thee shall prosper; and every tongue that shall rise against thee in judgment thou shalt condemn. This is the heritage of the servants of the Lord, and their righteousness is of Me, saith the Lord.

Matthew 5:44: But I say unto you, Love your enemies, bless them that curse you, do good to them that hate you, and pray for them which despitefully use you, and persecute you.

WHEN AN EMPLOYER WANTS TO HIRE YOU ON A TRIAL BASIS

Sometimes when you really want to get into a game, it doesn't matter to you what position the coach wants you to play as long as you get to play. And it is often the case that once you are sent in, your position may change to one you *really* want. All you have to do is play your very best and learn all you can about the game without being a hindrance to the coach or to the team.

The same strategy will benefit the job seeker who has been offered a position on a trial basis. If that's you, strongly consider allowing the employer to put you into the "game" —the company —in a position of his choosing. Once on board, work at your tasks as if you were the best paid employee in the place. Learn all you can so that you will be seen as far too valuable to release when the employer has to make a decision about whether or not to hire you.

You may be concerned that by accepting a position on a trial basis you are limiting your chances to be gainfully employed elsewhere. But you don't have to stop your search for permanent employment. During the negotiations for the trial job, indicate that while you are willing to demonstrate how well you can make a contribution to the company through your gratis work there, you will still need to find gainful employment. Ask to be allowed to leave an hour early here and there (always with notice) for interviewing. Indicate that you would also like to call employers during your lunch hours.

Remember that even when providing unpaid labor, we can still honor our Father—the real "Boss"—by performing our very best for His name's sake. Psalm 75:6, 7 makes a good case for still offering our best whether we are paid or not: *For promotion cometh neither from the east, nor from the west, nor from the south. But God is the judge: He putteth down one, and setteth up another.*

Power Scriptures for *When an Employer Wants to Hire You on a Trial Basis*

Job 8:7: Though thy beginning was small, yet thy later end should greatly increase.

Psalm 31:24: Be of good courage, and He shall strengthen your heart, all ye that hope in the Lord.

Psalm 107:37: And sow the fields, and plant vineyards, which may yield fruits of increase.

Psalm 115:14: The Lord shall increase you more and more, you and your children.

Proverbs 12:11a: He that tilleth his land shall be satisfied with bread.

Isaiah 65:23: They shall not labor in vain, nor bring forth for trouble; for they are the seed of the blessed of the Lord, and their offspring with them.

Daniel 6:3: Then this Daniel was preferred above the presidents and princes, because an excellent spirit was in him; and the king thought to set him over the whole realm.

Zechariah 8:12: For the seed shall be prosperous; the vine shall give her fruit, and the ground shall give her increase, and the heavens shall give their dew; and I will cause the remnant of this people to possess all these things.

Matthew 25:21: His lord said unto him, Well done, thou good and faithful servant: thou hast been faithful over a few things, I will make thee ruler over many things: enter thou into the joy of thy lord.

1 Corinthians 3:7, 8: So then neither is he that planteth any thing, neither he that watereth; but God that giveth the increase. Now he that planteth and he that watereth are one: and every man shall receive his own reward according to his own labor.

WHEN FACED WITH MORE THAN ONE JOB OFFER AT A TIME

While it is a potential blessing of God when we gain favor with more than one employer at a time, it also becomes our responsibility to be prayerful before God regarding our decision as to which employer to select. The second commandment presented in this book for a successful job search asks us to allow God to be our career counselor (see Section 2, Part 2). If we are committed to doing that, then when we begin to earnestly pray over our decisions, we may sense that one employer seems to "stand out" to us more than another. However, that kind of discernment, that kind of sensing an impression of God on the inside for decision-making, requires spending time alone with Him, with a high degree of consistency, before having to make a decision.

One of the employers may press you for a decision, and your mounting bills may do the same. Calm your mind and tell each employer making an offer that you need time (state a time frame: 24 hours, over the weekend, etc.) to make a decision—being very careful to communicate that you are interested. Then in solitude, join yourself to God in prayer to seek his guidance.

If after you have prayed, you still don't discern God's will in selecting one employer over another, apply Luke 14:28: *For which of you, intending to build a tower, sitteth not down first, and counteth the cost, whether he have sufficient to finish it?*

For our purposes here, counting the cost means studying each employer to see which of the positions best suits you and your abilities. For instance, ask yourself which best uses your strongest skills; which has an environment you would fit well in; which has a history of success; etc. Select the "winner," and make a call to accept one job — and a call to the other employer to decline.

Finally, despite which job you select, *believe God* for success in faith.

Power Scriptures for *When Faced with More Than One Job Offer At a Time*

Isaiah 48:17: Thus saith the Lord, thy Redeemer, the Holy One of Israel; I am the Lord thy God which teacheth thee to profit, which leadeth thee by the way that thou shouldest go.

Proverbs 3:6: In all thy ways acknowledge Him, and He shall direct thy paths.

Proverbs 11:14: Where no counsel is, the people fall: but in the multitude of counselors there is safety.

Proverbs 16:3: Commit thy works unto the Lord, and thy thoughts shall be established.

Psalm 32:8: I will instruct thee and teach thee in the way which thou shalt go: I will guide thee with Mine eye.

Psalm 37:23: The steps of a good man are ordered by the Lord: and He delighteth in his way.

Psalm 48:14: For this God is our God for ever and ever: He will be our guide even unto death.

Psalm 50:14: Offer unto God thanksgiving; and pay thy vows unto the most High.

Psalm 71:1: In Thee, O Lord, do I put my trust: let me never be put to confusion.

Psalm 143:8: Cause me to hear thy loving kindness in the morning; for in thee do I trust: cause me to know the way wherein I should walk; for I lift up my soul unto Thee.

Isaiah 50:7: For the Lord God will help me; therefore shall I not be confounded: therefore have I set my face like a flint, and I know that I shall not be ashamed.

1 Corinthians 7:20: Let every man abide in the same calling wherein he was called.

1 Corinthians 1:4: Now there are diversities of gifts, but the same Spirit.

1 Peter 2:6: Wherefore also it is contained in the scripture, Behold, I lay in Zion a chief corner stone, elect, precious: and he that believeth on Him shall not be confounded.

2 Peter 1:10: Wherefore the rather, brethren, give diligence to make your calling and election sure: for if ye do these things, ye shall never fall.

WHEN THE JOB OFFERED
IS NOT THE ONE DESIRED

When an employer asks a job candidate to take a position other than the one he applied for, often it is because something about the candidate came out during the interview that told the interviewer that the applicant would fare well in the alternative position. If we as job seekers find ourselves with an offer on the table for a job for which we did not apply, we must not be too quick to presume we are getting the short end of the stick and stomp off to search elsewhere. Sometimes great treasures come in unexpected packages.

We should first ask God for wisdom and guidance, then, assuming all systems are go on the inside of us, so to speak, we can give the alternative position a shot. More than likely, once we get on board, we will discover skills that we had all along but which always took a back seat to what we habitually considered our stronger skills.

There once was a degreed job seeker who applied at a hospital in a major city to work in its human resources department. But the interviewer offered her a job as a receptionist in the hospital's lab. She had no interest in laboratories or what was accomplished there, but she did love greeting people, answering telephones, typing, and having variety in her daily workload. So rather than stomping away from the opportunity at the thought of being offered a position "beneath" her skill level —after all, she had a degree!—she accepted instead. Not much later, she was able to transfer into the hospital's human resources department, her originally desired position, in response to an *internal* job posting. She found the good in that first offer, even saw beyond it, got in the door and succeeded.

See the possibilities *in back of* the current position you are being asked to fill. The job on the table now just may be the one that is in God's plan to move you to where He needs you to be in the near or distant future.

Power Scriptures for *When the Job Offered Is Not the One Desired*

Psalm 18:32: It is God that girdeth me with strength, and maketh my way perfect.

Psalm 31:24: Be of good courage, and He shall strengthen your heart, all ye that hope in the Lord.

Psalm 37:3: Trust in the Lord, and do good; so shalt thou dwell in the land, and verily thou shalt be fed.

Psalm 75:6, 7: For promotion cometh neither from the east, nor from the west, nor from the south. But God is the judge: he putteth down one, and setteth up another.

Proverbs 22:29: Seest thou a man diligent in his business? he shall stand before kings; he shall not stand before mean men.

Proverbs 28:1b: ...but the righteous are bold as a lion.

Isaiah 30:21: And thine ears shall hear a word behind thee, saying, This is the way, walk ye in it, when ye turn to the right hand, and when ye turn to the left.

Isaiah 48:17: Thus saith the Lord, thy Redeemer, the Holy One of Israel; I am the Lord thy God which teacheth thee to profit, which leadeth thee by the way that thou shouldest go.

Jeremiah 32:27: Behold, I am the Lord, the God of all flesh: is there any thing too hard for Me?

Romans 8:28: Cause me to hear Thy loving kindness in the morning; for in Thee do I trust: cause me to know the way wherein I should walk; for I lift up my soul unto Thee.

Acts 4:13: Now when they saw the boldness of Peter and John, and perceived that they were unlearned and ignorant men, they marveled; and they took knowledge of them, that they had been with Jesus.

2 Corinthians 8:12: For if there be first a willing mind, it is accepted according to that a man hath, and not according to that he hath not.

Philippians 4:13: I can do all things through Christ which strengtheneth me.

Colossians 3:23, 24: And whatsoever ye do, do it heartily, as to the Lord, and not unto men; knowing that of the Lord ye shall receive the reward of the inheritance: for ye serve the Lord Christ.

WHEN PERSONAL CALAMITIES THREATEN CONTINUED EMPLOYMENT ONCE HIRED

Life has a remarkable and consistent twist to it: after something wonderful happens to us, that positive event is sometimes followed by a negative event. For instance, you may be filled with joy one minute over having accepted an employer's offer of a new job and then find yourself ten minutes later lamenting over a phone call that just told you that due to a family member's illness, you will be required to provide personal attention daily, in conflict with your new work hours.

When sudden calamities happen to you that threaten your new job, your first thought may be to curse your "bad luck." Instead, assess the gravity of the situation in an unemotional frame of mind to discover what is actually required of your time. Next, plan a strategy for communicating your scheduling challenges to both your new boss and your family members. The worse thing you can do is to leave your new employer to speculate as to why you are late every day or are otherwise not pulling your full workload. He or she may also begin to wonder about his or her wisdom in having hired you.

You could offer ways to make up for any lost time and/or poor or low productivity. For instance, you could suggest a willingness to come in before or after hours or during the weekend. Or perhaps it may be possible for you to be allowed to work on projects at home until the crisis passes. What about offering to work an alternate shift? The point is, you do not have to lose an employment opportunity due to a personal setback. Talk about it, and be willing to ask for flexibility by the employer while offering to meet it with your own.

Should you find yourself immersed in a personal crisis after accepting a new job, take heart in knowing that God was aware that your attention would be drawn away from your new position long before you were offered the position, and that He had made a way for you to escape the trouble (see 1 Corinthians 10:13 below).

Power Scriptures for *When Personal Calamities Threaten Continued Employment Once Hired*

Psalm 34:19: Many are the afflictions of the righteous: but the Lord delivereth him out of them all.

Psalm 46:1: God is our refuge and strength, a very present help in trouble.

Psalm 57:1: Be merciful unto me, O God, be merciful unto me: for my soul trusteth in Thee: yea, in the shadow of Thy wings will I make my refuge, until these calamities be overpast.

Psalm 71:12: O God, be not far from me: O my God, make haste for my help.

Isaiah 40:29: He giveth power to the faint; and to them that have no might He increaseth strength.

Isaiah 41:10: Fear thou not; for I am with thee: be not dismayed; for I am thy God: I will strengthen thee; yea, I will help thee; yea, I will uphold thee with the right hand of my righteousness.

Isaiah 54:17: No weapon that is formed against thee shall prosper; and every tongue that shall rise against thee in judgment thou shalt condemn. This is the heritage of the servants of the Lord, and their righteousness is of Me, saith the Lord.

1 Corinthians 10:13: There hath no temptation taken you but such as is common to man: but God is faithful, who will not suffer you to be tempted above that ye are able; but will with the temptation also make a way to escape, that ye may be able to bear it.

Ephesians 6:11: Put on the whole armor of God, that ye may be able to stand against the wiles of the devil.

Hebrews 2:18: For in that He Himself hath suffered being tempted, He is able to succor them that are tempted.

James 1:2, 3: My brethren, count it all joy when ye fall into divers temptations; Knowing this, that the trying of your faith worketh patience.

James 1:12-14: Blessed is the man that endureth temptation…. Let no man say when he is tempted, I am tempted of God: for God cannot be tempted with evil, neither tempteth He any man: But every man is tempted, when he is drawn away of his own lust, and enticed.

WHEN WANTING TO START YOUR OWN BUSINESS

If after prayerful consideration, you still want to press forward to open your own business, it can only help to study books relevant to successful entrepreneurship to see how to best prepare for your success. Such books are available in abundance at most bookstores, and/or related information can be found on the Internet. Also, consider your responses to the following:

1) Are you following the leading of God? One way you'll know you are being led is that you will experience a strong peace over your decision.

2) Does your business put your best skills, attributes, personality tendencies, talents, interests, and desires to work?

3) Have you written your vision so plainly that anyone reading it understands what your business is all about (see Habakkuk 2:2 below) and can see how you plan to make and sustain profit?

4) Is yours a *godly* business? For we Christians, who are called Ambassadors of Christ, are required to put our hands to appropriate work. That's hard to do if we know ahead of time that the intended use of our end-products may bring harm to our potential consumers.

5) Are you (or will you be) surrounded by wise counsel? Have you gotten feedback about your idea from other than "yes" people?

6) Are you as bold as a lion? Boldness is a *required* trait of entrepreneurs.

7) Are you willing to work very long hours for at least the first couple of years?

Remember that according to Ecclesiastes 5:3: *...a dream cometh through the multitude of business* —or a lot of hard work! So be certain of your commitment level; and know that with God, all things are possible. Allow Him to be your business partner.

Power Scriptures for *When Wanting to Start Your Own Business*

Judges 18:5: And they said unto him, Ask counsel, we pray thee, of God, that we may know whether our way which we go shall be prosperous.

Proverbs 3:5, 6: Trust in the Lord with all thine heart; and lean not unto thine own understanding. In all thy ways acknowledge Him, and He shall direct thy paths.

Proverbs 8:21: That I may cause those that love Me to inherit substance; and I will fill their treasures.

Proverbs 11:14: Where no counsel is, the people fall: but in the multitude of counselors there is safety.

Isaiah 30:21: And thine ears shall hear a word behind thee, saying, This is the way, walk ye in it, when ye turn to the right hand, and when ye turn to the left.

Isaiah 64:8: ...O Lord, Thou art our Father; we are the clay, and Thou our potter; and we all are the work of Thy hand.

Proverbs 28:1b: ...but the righteous are bold as a lion.

Jeremiah 10:23: O Lord, I know that the way of man is not in himself: it is not in man that walketh to direct his steps.

Jeremiah 32:27: Behold, I am the Lord, the God of all flesh: is there any thing too hard for Me?

Habakkuk 2:2: And the Lord answered me, and said, Write the vision, and make it plain upon tables, that he may run that readeth it.

Luke 14:28: For which of you, intending to build a tower, sitteth not down first, and counteth the cost, whether he have sufficient to finish it?

1 Corinthians 7:22: For he that is called in the Lord, being a servant, is the Lord's freeman: likewise also he that is called, being free, is Christ's servant.

1 Corinthians 9:19: For though I be free from all men, yet have I made myself servant unto all, that I might gain the more.

1 Peter 2:16: As free, and not using your liberty for a cloak of maliciousness, but as the servants of God.

3 John 1:2: Beloved, I wish above all things that thou mayest prosper and be in health, even as thy soul prospereth.

Revelation 3:8: I know thy works: behold, I have set before thee an open door, and no man can shut it: for thou hast a little strength, and hast kept My word, and hast not denied My name.

WHEN ANTICIPATING THE FIRST DAY ON YOUR NEW JOB

The Bible teaches us that when we pray for anything, including new jobs, that due to the godliness of the request (you see, we don't pray for foolish, ungodly things), we believe we will receive answers; and we are to act like we believe. I trust that after praying for a new job, you have already taken action: you built your resume, you are practicing your interviewing technique, you are following this book's "commandments" for a successful job search to your best ability, and you have prayed and are now standing in faith, believing God for work.

As you continue to believe God for work and press your way toward the goal of employment in faith, pray also for your yet-unknown co-workers, bosses, and new company. Doing so is a way of acting on what you believe —that you will win employment (remembering that faith without corresponding action is faith applied to nothing). By praying for your new position before you get it, you fortify yourself for the new, the unknown.

What follows is a variety of scriptures for meditation that I trust will encourage and strengthen you for the first day you arrive at your new worksite. May God be with you and continually bless your journey forward. And may you be ever mindful of his promise in Matthew 28:20b: ...*lo, I am with you always even unto the end of the world.*

Power Scriptures for *When Anticipating the First Day on Your New Job*

Genesis 18:4a: Is anything too hard for the Lord?

Deuteronomy 8:11: Beware that thou forget not the Lord thy God, in not keeping His commandments, and His judgments, and His statutes, which I command thee this day.

Deuteronomy 1:21: Behold, the Lord thy God hath set the land before thee: go up and possess it, as the Lord God of thy fathers hath said unto thee; fear not, neither be discouraged.

Numbers 13:30b: Let us go up at once, and possess it; for we are well able to overcome it.

Proverbs 3:3, 4: Let not mercy and truth forsake thee: bind them about thy neck; write them upon the table of thine heart: So shalt thou find favor and good understanding in the sight of God and man.

Proverbs 12:11: He that tilleth his land shall be satisfied with bread: but he that followeth vain persons is void of understanding.

Proverbs 18:24: A man that hath friends must show himself friendly.

Isaiah 26:3: Thou will keep his mind in perfect peace, whose mind is stayed on Thee: because he trusteth in Thee.

Luke 1:12: For the Holy Ghost shall teach you in the same hour what ye ought to say.

John 12:26: If any man serve Me, let him follow Me; and where I am, there shall also my servant be: if any man serve Me, him will my Father honor.

Romans 13:3, 4a: For rulers are not a terror to good works, but to the evil. Wilt thou then not be afraid of the power? do that which is good, and thou shalt have praise of the same: for He is the minister of God to thee for good.

Romans 8:16: The Spirit itself beareth witness with our spirit, that we are the children of God.

1 Corinthians 13:1: Though I speak with the tongues of men and of angels, and have not charity [love], I am become as sounding brass, or a tinkling cymbal.

Colossians 3:23: And whatsoever ye do, do it heartily, as to the Lord, and not unto men.

2 Thessalonians 2:16, 17: Now our Lord Jesus Christ Himself, and God, even our Father, which hath loved us, and hath given us everlasting consolation and good hope through grace, comfort your hearts, and establish you in every good word *and work*.

1 Timothy 2:1, 2: I exhort therefore, that, first of all, supplications, prayers, intercessions, and giving of thanks be made for all men; for kings, and for all that are in authority; that we may lead a quiet and peaceable life in all godliness and honesty.

Revelation 22:12: ...behold I come quickly and my reward is with Me to give every man according as his work [effort, deed, occupation] shall be.

- **An event that is heavily steeped in strategy**

    The interviewer can use any number of tactics (i.e., the pressure or "stress" interview, the performance interview, the "power-lunch" interview, etc.) in order to learn about your personality and the depth of your experience. A wise job applicant is armed with his own strategy (i.e., thinking like an employer or business owner, anticipating the interviewer's needs, etc.). Confident and courageous, this applicant listens for opportunities in each question to position himself to win the job.

- **Similar to a game of chess or cards —and not one of ping-pong**

  A ping-pong style of interviewing is one in which a job applicant responds to questions so briefly that an outside observer could liken the exchange between the interviewer and the applicant to a game of ping pong. It goes something like this: the interviewer asks a question—the applicant sends maybe two short sentences back to him in response. The interviewer re-phrases the question because the response lacked substance; but the applicant knocks a response right back across the desk with words as empty as the first response. Ping-pong responses from an applicant signal loud and clear that he has little to offer. He may not be a "closed door" (as described above) in the sense that he may at least be welcoming and friendly, but his ping-pong style of responding to questions makes the interviewing process extremely frustrating. The employer can hear an applicant's lack of self-study in this kind of rapid, back and forth style of communicating.

An applicant who has conducted that all-important self-research not only avoids verbal ping-pong, but he is free to present himself in a way that more closely resembles a game of chess or even cards. He plays "chess", for instance, by thinking several moves ahead of the interviewer. That is, he considers the rationale behind each question *before* answering. He plays "cards" by "laying down" only the kind of information that is most pertinent to the question that's "on the table." He reserves information (keeps his cards close to his chest, as it were) for the most strategic time to "play" (share) the information —or he may decide to "hold" information for when he's invited to a second interview. Further, he wisely understands that everything in his "hand" does not need to be revealed (i.e., details to his personal life and/or all of the working experience, good or bad, he's ever had). Instead, he simply "follows suit" after the interviewer and provides responses that are pertinent and substantial. His are not empty, useless ping-pong-ball words. The interview starts to pick up purposeful momentum rather than remaining a stagnant event that becomes frustrating for both sides.

What an Interviewer Seeks

Very basically, an interviewer seeks someone who will fit in, do the work well, and not cause any grief. So during the interview he listens intently to hear *the depth of the value inside* of what is being shared in response to his questions. And for anyone trying to make a wise hiring decision, there is a huge difference between a job applicant who responds to *"Tell me about yourself"*, for instance, by saying *"I am dependable and productive"* and one who says, *"I can be counted upon to maintain a high work ethic –I believe in giving 100% effort for the pay; I am a team-player who believes in pulling my share of the weight, and look forward to contributing to the company's goals."* Which of the two would *you* hire if you were the employer? Probably the second applicant. He did not depend upon the employer to define "dependable" and "productive" *for him* as the first applicant did.

Lastly, I offer now a simple formula, *G+L/LoS*, to help you understand the importance of choosing the right words to feed on and/or to communicate during the job search process. *G+L/LoS* is an abbreviated way of stating: **G**oal plus **L**anguage will determine the **L**ikelihood **o**f **S**uccess for achieving said goal.

What follows are three examples of *L* (language) used by two "job seekers" to demonstrate how word choice can contribute to their *LoS* (likelihood of success) in winning the *G* (goal) of employment.

Job Seeker #1: *G* = Employment   **Job Seeker #2:** *G* = Employment

Ex. A

L: "I'll never find a job." > **LoS = low.**   *L*: "Someone, somewhere will want to hire me!" > **LoS = high.**

Ex. B

L: "Well, Sir –I want to work for your company because I need medical   *L*: "Well, Sir – I want to work here because I believe my skills, this benefits —income for bills." > **LoS = low.**

position, and this company all match. And here's why..." > **LoS = high.**

Ex. C

L: "I *am* a good worker!" > **LoS = low.**

L: "Yes, I am a good worker. For instance, you can count on me to..." > **LoS = high.**

Example A shows two instances of self-speak job seekers can feed on.

Of the two, which job seeker do you think will continue to job search for as long as it takes to reach *G*–employment? More than likely you'd agree that Job Seeker #2 has a higher likelihood of success (*LoS*). It is difficult to convince yourself to commit to anything while at the same time confessing defeat about it. A strong commitment to winning employment over the long haul is crucial in tough economic times, such as now, where the job market is highly competitive. What is your self-speak like? Does it add to or subtract from your *LoS*?

Example B shows two different responses to the interview question "Why do you want to work for us?" Does Job Seeker #2 stand out as someone who avoids giving pat, scripted, ping-pong answers? Do you see why his *LoS* is higher for reaching his *G* of employment than is Job Seeker #1's *LoS*?

In our last example, C, notice how Job Seeker #1 provides a fairly impressive response to "Are you a good worker?" If you were the employer, wouldn't you be even more impressed with the second job seeker's response? When you compare the two responses in *Example C* (as an employer inevitably would compare candidates' responses after a day of interviewing), notice how Job Seeker #2 was ready to provide *examples* to help the interviewer hear that he had experience in being a good worker.

In sum, remember that interviewing is likened to a game of chess or cards or any game that requires multi-level, strategic thinking. (One could argue that ping-pong also requires a strategy in order to win. Does it require the level of strategizing that chess and cards require? Or is it mostly reactive?) The interview is a treasure hunt for you to seek out the right job —to get yourself seated in your calling. There are people you have yet to meet who may need the God-given abilities planted inside of you. Make it your business to ask two questions of any employer who turns you down:

1) *Is there anything I could improve upon for the next time I interview?*

2) *Do you know of other positions opening up at this or another company for which you believe I may be suited?*

Finally, always remember that your not being chosen for the job after an interview doesn't automatically mean you weren't being strongly considered. Often, it is because you did do well that an employer might be willing to steer you to someone else he knows is hiring —and will allow you to use his name to get in the door to boot! Just gather your courage after each interview, and *ask*!

NOTES